EDWARD GIBBON
THE HISTORIAN

By the same author

BEGINNING THE TWENTIETH CENTURY

THE ANCIENT WORLD

THE HARPER HISTORY OF CIVILIZATION

THE PEOPLES OF THE ANCIENT WORLD
(*with W. H. Armstrong*)

Edward Gibbon in 1774

EDWARD GIBBON THE HISTORIAN

BY

JOSEPH WARD SWAIN, PH.D.

Formerly Chairman of the Department of History, University of Illinois

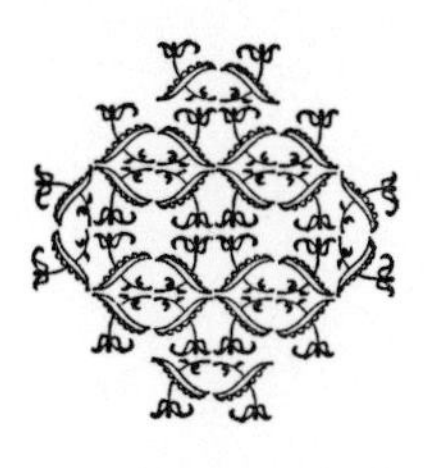

MACMILLAN: London, Melbourne & Toronto.

ST MARTIN'S PRESS: New York.

1966

MACMILLAN AND COMPANY LIMITED
Little Essex Street London WC 2
also Bombay Calcutta Madras Melbourne

THE MACMILLAN COMPANY OF CANADA LIMITED
70 Bond Street Toronto 2

ST MARTIN'S PRESS INC
175 *Fifth Avenue New York NY* 10010

Library of Congress catalog card no. 66–22809

PRINTED IN GREAT BRITAIN

To Margaret

WITH LOVE AND ADMIRATION

CONTENTS

ILLUSTRATIONS

ACKNOWLEDGEMENTS

I MUST express my indebtedness to many persons. First of all I am grateful to the three scholars — the English D. M. Low and Miss J. E. Norton, and the Swiss Georges Bonnard — whose recent splendid editions of the historian's letters and journals have done so much to advance Gibbon studies, and to A. L. Rowse, of All Souls College, Oxford, for much timely aid and encouragement. I am also grateful to the librarians of the University of Illinois Library, of the Huntington Library, and of the Yale University Library for helpful assistance. The British Museum has supplied microfilms of many unpublished papers in its possession. And I am especially indebted to the trustees of the Huntington Library, in San Marino, California, for their generous grant in aid, which enabled me to work for several months amid beautiful surroundings and in an inspiring company of scholars.

The genealogical table is based on two tables published in D. M. Low's *Edward Gibbon*, 1737–1794 (Chatto & Windus, London, 1937).

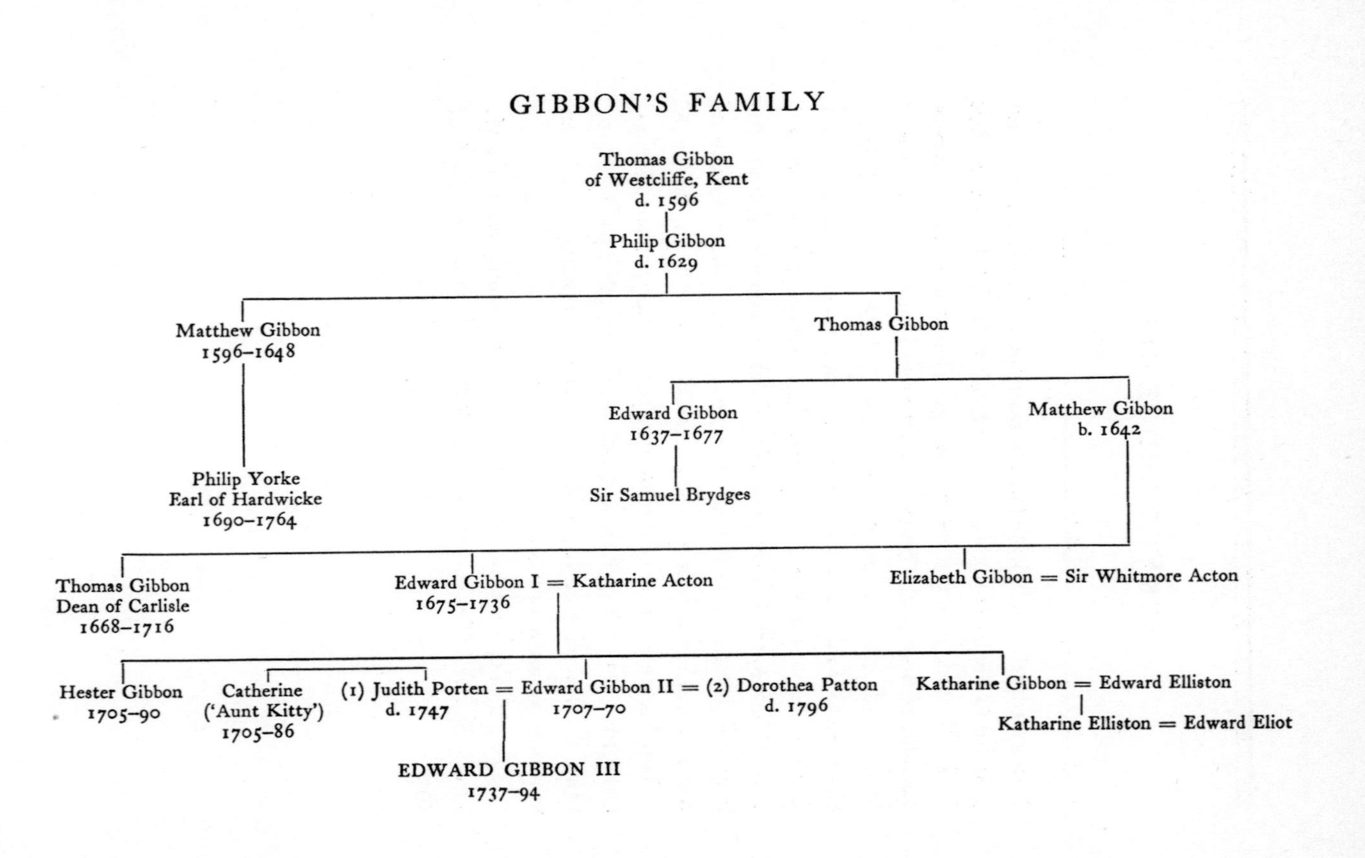
GIBBON'S FAMILY
Thomas Gibbon
of Westcliffe, Kent
d. 1596
Philip Gibbon
d. 1629
Matthew Gibbon
1596–1648
Thomas Gibbon
Edward Gibbon
1637–1677
Matthew Gibbon
b. 1642
Philip Yorke
Earl of Hardwicke
1690–1764
Sir Samuel Brydges
Thomas Gibbon
Dean of Carlisle
1668–1716
Edward Gibbon I = Katharine Acton
1675–1736
Elizabeth Gibbon = Sir Whitmore Acton
Hester Gibbon
1705–90
Catherine
('Aunt Kitty')
1705–86
(1) Judith Porten = Edward Gibbon II = (2) Dorothea Patton
d. 1747
1707–70
d. 1796
Katharine Gibbon = Edward Elliston
Katharine Elliston = Edward Eliot
EDWARD GIBBON III
1737–94

GIBBON'S CHRONOLOGY

1737 8 May. Born at Putney.

1752 April. Enters Oxford.

1753 Converted to Catholicism; leaves Oxford; sent to Lausanne.

1754 Returns to Protestantism.

1757 Meets Suzanne Curchod: 'I saw and loved.'

1758 April. Returns to England.

1760 May–December 1762. Active service in militia.

1761 March. Stands for Parliament, but withdraws before vote is taken.

July. Publishes his *Essai*.

1763 January–May. First visit to Paris.

May–April 1764. Second visit to Lausanne.

1764 April–April 1765. In Italy.

2 October. Reaches Rome.

1765–72 Divides time between London and Buriton.

1768 Starts and abandons *History of Switzerland*.

1770 Attacks Warburton's interpretation of Virgil.

Father dies.

1772 Settles in London.

1774 Joins Literary Club.

1774–80 M.P. for Liskeard.

1776 February. Publishes vol. 1 of *The Decline and Fall*.

American Declaration of Independence: Gibbon supports Lord North.

1777 May–October. Second visit to Paris.

17 October. Burgoyne surrenders: Gibbon critical of North.

1778 January–February. Votes with Fox in Parliament.

February. Franco-American alliance: England and France at war.

1779	July. Appointed to Board of Trade
	October. *Mémoire justificatif.*
1780	February. Gibbon attacked by opposition: Burke introduces his 'Economical Reform Bill', but later withdraws it.
	September. Eliot refuses to continue Gibbon as M.P. for Liskeard.
1781	March. Vols. II and III of *The Decline and Fall* published.
1781–4	M.P. for Lymington.
1782	March. North ministry falls.
	July. Board of Trade abolished.
1783	Writes vol. IV of *The Decline and Fall.*
	September. Withdraws to Lausanne.
1784–23	June 1787. Writes vols. V and VI.
1788	In London to oversee printing of vols. IV, V, and VI: returns to Lausanne.
1788–93	Writes six fragments of Memoirs.
1793	Returns to England.
1794	16 January. Dies in London.
1796	Lord Sheffield publishes Gibbon's *Memoirs.*

CHAPTER ONE

MR. GIBBON WRITES HIS MEMOIRS

IT was at Rome, on an October evening in 1764, that Edward Gibbon first conceived the idea of writing the history of the decline and fall of the Roman Empire, but not until almost twenty-three years later did he complete his self-imposed task. This consummation of his life-work came at Lausanne, in Switzerland, on a June evening in 1787. Much had happened to the historian and to the world during the quarter of a century that separated these two memorable evenings, but perseverance and determination at last brought Gibbon to the hour of his final deliverance. In a highly poetic passage of his Memoirs he describes that hour.

> It was on the day, or rather the night, of the 27th of June, 1787, between the hours of eleven and twelve, that I wrote the last lines of the last page in a summer-house in my garden. After laying down my pen I took several turns in a *berceau*, or covered walk of Acacias, which commands a prospect of the country, the lake, and the mountains. The air was temperate, the sky was serene, the silver orb of the moon was reflected from the waters, and all Nature was silent. I will not dissemble the first emotions of joy on the recovery of my freedom, and perhaps the establishment of my fame. But my pride was soon humbled, and a sober melancholy was spread over my mind by the idea that I had taken an everlasting leave of an old and agreable companion . . .[1]

Even then, however, Gibbon's task was not completed. The printing of his last three volumes required his presence in London, and it was with trepidation that he returned to his native land. He had been somewhat under a cloud, both socially and politically, when he left England in 1783, and his four years in Lausanne had been a voluntary exile.[2] He might well wonder what sort of a reception he would receive in England. His fears were unjustified, however, for the old quarrels were now forgotten, and everything went smoothly. When the concluding volumes of his History appeared — on 8 May 1788, the historian's fifty-first birthday — critics and public alike greeted them with the same high praise that had been lavished upon their predecessors. Gibbon's fame was secure, and he knew that he had won a place among the world's great historians.

During his visit to London Gibbon was the recipient of other honours as well. He was named Professor of Ancient History at the Royal Academy (a signal though empty distinction); at a banquet in his honour he listened enraptured to the reading of an ode whose author bracketed him with Shakespeare and Newton as one of England's three outstanding geniuses. Sitting in the crowded gallery during the trial of Warren Hastings (the *cause célèbre* of the day) he enjoyed the immense satisfaction of hearing the prosecutor (R. B. Sheridan) shout, towards the climax of a brilliant denunciation of Hastings for his dealings with the Begum of Oudh, that 'nothing equal in criminality was to be traced either in ancient or modern history, in the correct periods of Tacitus or the luminous page of Gibbon'. And he was invited to dine with the Prince of Wales. Friends and acquaintances urged him to re-establish his residence in London, but Gibbon believed that he would be happier at Lausanne, and in July 1788 he returned to Switzerland.

Gibbon passed the remaining years of his life quietly and contentedly at Lausanne. Here he moved in the best Swiss society, and, as the city lay on the route usually followed by English travellers making the Grand Tour, he often received visitors from England. Much as he enjoyed these social diversions, however, they were not enough to satisfy him, and he soon was seeking more creative pastimes. At first he occupied his new leisure by reading and re-

reading the Greek and Latin classics, but after a few months he began to work on the book which became his second masterpiece — his *Memoirs of My Life and Writings*.

The idea of writing an autobiography was suggested to Gibbon by a gift from a chance acquaintance. In 1784 a young German prince arrived in Lausanne, accompanied by his tutor, E. T. Langer. This tutor had met Gibbon in London a few years before, and at Lausanne the two men resumed friendly relations. After his return to Germany in 1786 Langer sent Gibbon a little book on heraldry, entitled *Introductio ad Latinam Blasoniam*, by a certain John Gibbon, a member of the Heralds Office, who had lived in the seventeenth century.[3] In this booklet the herald traced his ancestry to a fourteenth-century family of Gibbons of Rolvenden, in Kent, and through them he claimed relationship by marriage with several aristocratic families, notably with the barons of Saye and Sele. Gibbon was delighted by this discovery. From his youth upwards he had thirsted for fame and had hoped to be accepted by the society of his day as a man of fashion as well as a man of letters, as a gentleman as well as a scholar, but his efforts to shine in London society had led only to ridicule. Now, however, a delectable prospect suddenly opened before his eyes. If only he could prove himself related to this John Gibbon, he could boast of family connections more ancient and more honourable than those of many of the persons by whom he had been snubbed or insultingly patronized during his difficult years in London.

Doing a little research of his own, Gibbon read (in Shakespeare[4]) that the first Baron of Saye and Sele, whom he now claimed as an ancestor in the eleventh degree, had been beheaded by Jack Cade, who accused him of various crimes, including selling Maine and Normandy to the Dauphin of France, speaking Latin, erecting a grammar school, and setting up a printing press. 'Of some of these meritorious crimes,' commented Gibbon, 'I should hope to find my ancestor guilty; and a man of letters may be proud of his descent from a Patron and martyr of learning.'

As he was then deeply engaged in writing the last chapters of his History, Gibbon had no time for further genealogical researches, but when he returned to England a year later he made a few desultory efforts to learn more about his family. Until this time he had cared little for, and known nothing of, his ancestors beyond his grandfather, but he now discovered that his grandfather was the son of Matthew Gibbon, a linen draper of London. The historian then decided (quite without evidence) that this Matthew (born 1642) must be a younger brother of John Gibbon the herald (born 1629). He therefore claimed as his own all the ancestors whom John had mentioned. Without more ado he set himself up as a man of family, at least to the extent of blazoning John Gibbon's arms on a bookplate that he ordered engraved at this time.[5]

This welcome discovery of distinguished ancestors, quickly followed by his flattering literary and social triumphs at London, suggested to Gibbon that he write an autobiography. He could thus parade his newly found ancestors before the world and he could show how he had arranged his whole life with a view to producing his great History: nothing else, he would show, had really mattered. Shortly after his return to Lausanne he began writing.[6] He found the task difficult, however, and during the next three years he composed six different drafts of an autobiography. None of these satisfied him and only one carried the story beyond his father's death in 1770. Each draft began with an account of his early ancestors, taken from John Gibbon; this was followed by sketches of his grandfather and father, based on family tradition and personal recollection; and lastly came Gibbon's story of his own youth, drawn largely from memory, but supported by a few letters and by a journal, which he had kept from 1761 to 1764. Being a careful historian, Gibbon knew that personal memory and family tradition are not the most solid foundations for a historical narrative, and that he must therefore make further researches in England before he could write a definitive version of his autobiography. He then arranged to visit Lord Sheffield in the autumn of 1792 (he actually

Thomas Gibbon. of Westcliffe early in Q. Eliz
died 1596

Philip. died. 1629 — 1585 — Elizabeth Philpot died 1647. aged 80

Matthew died 1629. aged 72.

Dorothy Best died 1634 — Thomas Gibbon born 1590. died 1671 — Alice Netherton

Matthew born 1596. died. 1648.

Thomas of Westcliffe sold in the be: ginning of this Century

Richard a Physician died 1652 one of eleven younger children of £1000 each

Edward born 1637

Matthew born. 1642.

Richard born 1627. died 1679

— Acton — Edward. S.S. Director born. 1667 died. 1736

Thomas Dean of Carlisle

Elizabeth born. 1658 died. 1727

Philip Yorke born 1651 died. 1721

Judith Porter — Edward. born 1707 Died. 1770

Hester Catherine

C. Elliston

Lord Chancellor Hardwicke born 1690

Edward born 1737

Lady Eliot

Gibbon's genealogy in his own handwriting

did not leave Lausanne until May 1793), laid his manuscripts aside, and began considering other literary projects, notably a 'History of the House of Brunswick', from which the Hanoverian kings of England were descended.

Then the heavens fell. Gibbon's distant and hitherto-unknown cousin, Sir Egerton Brydges, had likewise been investigating the Gibbon family history and had found that both he and the historian were descended, not from John Gibbon's family at Rolvenden in western Kent, but from a family of Gibbons at Westcliffe, near Dover in eastern Kent. Though Brydges published his version of the family genealogy anonymously in the *Gentleman's Magazine* for August 1788, Gibbon did not see his article until late in February 1792.[7] Realizing that Brydges's findings, if authenticated, would rob him of the ancestors of whom he had become so proud, Gibbon wrote that very day to the editor of the magazine to inquire about the author of this anonymous article. When he received no reply (the editor's two letters apparently were lost in the mails), he 'impatiently' wrote to Sheffield twice during the next few months, and once to another friend in London, requesting them to prod the editor into replying. Not until he reached London, more than a year later, did Gibbon learn the author's identity. He then wrote to Brydges, who supplied him with materials that enabled him to construct a correct family tree. Nevertheless, Gibbon was reluctant to surrender John — not to mention the Lord Saye and Sele whom Shakespeare had honoured so highly — and a new book-plate that he ordered at this time still blazoned John's arms. Indeed, it is not improbable that the two Gibbon families came eventually from a single stock, and that the historian really was entitled to use the Gibbon arms, but he certainly would have to surrender the various noble families to whom John claimed relationship on his mother's side — including Lord Saye and Sele.

All was not lost, however. Gibbon might lose his 'martyr of learning', who had been dead for upwards of three hundred years, but he won a hitherto unsuspected relative in Lord Hardwicke, an eminent Whig politician in the days of George II, who became lord chancellor and who is recognized today as one of England's great judges. This man, the first Lord Hardwicke (1690–1764), had known Gibbon's father slightly, and his son, the second earl, had been acquainted with Gibbon himself. In 1781 Gibbon presented him with copies of the second and third volumes of *The Decline and Fall* (though at this time he had no suspicion that he might be related to that family), and in return received a flattering letter of thanks and a book written by Hardwicke. The first Lord Hardwicke undoubtedly knew that his mother was a Gibbon, for when he was raised to the peerage (1733) he quartered the Gibbon family arms with his own.[8] Perhaps it did not occur to him that the rather unimportant Gibbon whom he knew (the historian's father) belonged to this family, or perhaps he decided that if the Gibbons did not know that they were related to him he would leave them in their ignorance. After all, he was now an earl and Gibbon was not, and he presumably felt himself to be under no obligation to take up with his obscure relatives. When Gibbon finally discovered his kinship with the Hardwickes he made no effort to establish contact with the third earl (who had inherited the title in 1790, and who was then British ambassador to the Netherlands), but he drew up a genealogical table showing the close connection of the two families, putting his name beside Hardwicke's, and doubly underlining eachs After Gibbon's death Lord Sheffield gave this paper, in Gibbon'. own handwriting, to the third Lord Hardwicke, and it is now preserved with the Hardwicke papers in the British Museum.[9]

Gibbon would certainly have altered the early pages of his Memoirs drastically — omitting John Gibbon and his ancestors and adding something about the Hardwickes — had he not died suddenly in London on 16 January 1794. His Will directed that Lord Sheffield, his executor, should publish whatever manuscripts might be found among his possessions. The most interesting and most important of these manuscripts were, of course, the six unfinished drafts of the Memoirs, and it devolved upon Lord Sheffield to prepare them for publication. With the aid of his brilliant daughter Maria and a few friends, he successfully wove the six drafts into one continuous narrative. He selected now one version and now another as his basic text, but he inserted phrases, sentences, or even whole paragraphs from other drafts when they added new facts or felicitous expressions. He deleted much that Gibbon had written, largely to avoid repetitions, but also to tone down ridiculously boastful passages, or to spare the feelings of persons still alive, or from mere prudery. He also added footnotes, some written by himself (and so labelled) and some taken from Gibbon's Journal. He added his own account of Gibbon's last days and appended 265 letters from or to Gibbon. This version of the Memoirs and letters was published in 1796 as the first volume of a quarto edition of Gibbon's *Miscellaneous Works*; a second volume, appearing at the same time, contained several of Gibbon's minor writings.

Eighteen years later, in 1814, Sheffield published a second edition of the *Miscellaneous Works* in five octavo volumes, introducing a few slight changes in the Memoirs, adding several letters, and including more of the minor works. Except for a few letters, nothing new appeared thereafter until 1894, when, on the centenary of Gibbon's death, all his papers were acquired by the British Museum. The six versions of the Memoirs were then printed exactly as they came from Gibbon's pen, and a new and fuller edition of the letters followed. Scholars were amazed when they discovered the extent of Sheffield's alteration of Gibbon's text, but, when they had recovered from their initial surprise, they admitted that he had performed his task remarkably well. He had made a literary masterpiece out of six disjointed fragments. Never in literary history has so delicate a task been more brilliantly performed.

Gibbon's Memoirs remain our principal source of information regarding his life, and if we bear in mind when, how, why, and under what circumstances they were written, we find them instructive as well as entertaining. In recent years, moreover, careful editions of Gibbon's letters and journals have been published, making it possible to check, rectify, or elaborate upon statements made in the Memoirs. Aside from his own writings, however, there is no great body of contemporary material regarding Gibbon, for the anecdotes reported by his contemporaries are usually of questionable authenticity. During his lifetime Gibbon was the victim of an exceptional amount of malicious gossip and slander, both in London and among the English who visited Lausanne. His odd appearance, his vanity and conceit, his elaborate overdressing, the French mannerisms, which he acquired in youth and never outgrew, all made him an easy target for jesters. He also had the misfortune to fall into disfavour with some of the ablest retailers of gossip in his day. Dr. Johnson dislike him, Boswell loathed him, Horace Walpole held him up to ridicule, and countless lesser wits followed in the train of these masters. Many of their stories were probably true, at least in part, but some of them have been proved false and others simply are not worth refuting.

CHAPTER TWO

A GENTLEMAN AND A SCHOLAR

EDWARD GIBBON the historian was the third member of his immediate family to bear that name. His grandfather, the first Edward Gibbon (1675–1736), was the son of Matthew Gibbon, a linen draper of London, who had left his native village in Kent and come up to the city in the days of King Charles II. After Matthew's death, in the early 1690s, his widow managed the prosperous business for several years while their son, Edward, was in Flanders acquiring a fortune by selling provisions to the British armies there. This Edward Gibbon's skill in business is attested by Lord Bolingbroke's remark that he had never conversed with a man who more clearly understood the commerce and finances of England.

During the last four years of Queen Anne's reign, when Bolingbroke and the Tories were in power (1710–14), this first Edward Gibbon held office as a commissioner of customs, and in 1716 he became a director of the notorious South Sea Company. This high honour led to his undoing, however, for when the 'South Sea Bubble' burst (1720) a vindictive Whig Parliament expropriated the personal property of the company's directors to indemnify its creditors. Gibbon's fortune amounted to more than £100,000, of which he was allowed to keep only £10,000; but he managed to secrete and save much more. Among the properties thus salvaged was a spacious house at Putney, then a fashionable suburb of London lying about five miles up the Thames from the heart of the City. Here the old man passed the remainder of his days, and here he died in 1736. During his last sixteen years he had accumulated a new fortune, not much inferior to the first, and he thus made it possible for his son to live at ease as a country gentleman and for his grandson to dedicate his life to scholarship.

The second Edward Gibbon (1707–70), like so many sons of rich and strong-willed fathers, grew up to be a pleasant and affable fellow who could converse easily with either a ploughman or a peer, but who was a spendthrift with no great strength of character. People liked him well enough, but they refused to take him seriously. As a boy he had been sent to the fashionable Westminster School — at that time Eton's chief rival as a playing-field for the sons of the British aristocracy — and though he matriculated at Emmanuel College, Cambridge, in 1723, he left the university seven years later without taking a degree. After a few months of travel in France he returned to Putney, where he presently committed his one recorded act of insubordination. In the face of his father's opposition he married Judith Porten, the daughter of a neighbour at Putney whose finances were in a rather shaky condition (1736). This disobedience caused his father to draw up a new Will, by which he left a little more of his wealth to his two daughters and a little less to his son (or so the son believed and the grandson wrote), and he entailed the estate in order to make sure that his wanton son would not mortgage or sell it and squander the proceeds.

When the elder Gibbon died, some seven months later, his son set himself up as a man of fortune. He and his socially ambitious wife attempted, quite unsuccessfully, to shine in London society.[1] They entertained lavishly and lost more than they could afford in gambling; he sat in Parliament as a Tory for thirteen years (1734–47); and for two years he was a London alderman (1743–5). People high in society accepted his hospitality and cheerfully pocketed the money he lost to them at cards, but they refused to consider him one of their social set. After his wife's death (23 February 1747) he abandoned these social ambitions, leased the house at Putney to a tenant, and withdrew to a country estate at Buriton in Hampshire, about sixty miles south of London. Here he lived in some style and quite beyond his means until his death in 1770.

His son, the historian, was born at Putney on 8 May 1737, the first of seven children and the only one to survive infancy. He was a sickly boy, afflicted with one grave illness after another, badly treated by incompetent physicians, and neglected by his parents. As his mother's highest ambition in those days was to cut a fine figure in London society, her life was fully occupied in a ceaseless round of social functions, and she had little time for her son, who owed his life to the devoted care of his 'Aunt Kitty' — his mother's sister, Miss Catherine Porten. She it was who watched over him in his cradle, often fearing that each hour would be his last, and later it was she who taught him the rudiments of reading and religion. He repaid her with affection and esteem until her death in 1786, and his Memoirs contain an eloquent tribute to her goodness.[2]

The boy's health being what it was, regular schooling was out of the question. At first he was placed under the tutelage of a local clergyman; later he passed a few months in a small school where 'at the expense of many tears and some blood I purchased the knowledge of the Latin syntax'; and, after his mother's death, he was sent to his father's old school, Westminster (January 1748). In selecting this school, the father undoubtedly was thinking of the aristocratic contacts his son could make at Westminster rather than of the intellectual training he might receive. Many of the boy's schoolmates came from socially distinguished families, it is true, but young Gibbon formed no lasting friendships among them. His long illnesses had left him too weak for their rough games; he was bookish and had peculiar ideas of his own; and the other boys left him to himself. His continued sickness caused him to be withdrawn from Westminster (August 1750), and again he was placed under a private tutor. When this tutor proved unsatisfactory, the father in desperation entered his son at Magdalen College, Oxford (April 1752). The boy was then a few days under fifteen years of age.

Gibbon's mind had not been dormant during these difficult years, for under the guidance of his aunt, 'the true mother of my mind as well as of my health', he had learned to take a deep delight in books. Like many imaginative youngsters he enjoyed the *Arabian Nights*, and he eagerly devoured Pope's translation of Homer and Dryden's Virgil. When his grandfather Porten fell into bankruptcy and absconded (1747), the boy was given the free run of his library, which was rich in works of romance, history, and travel. As Porten had been interested in the Turkey trade, his library doubtless contained books which whetted his grandson's curiosity about the exotic Near East, while others carried him to China or Peru. Gibbon continued this undirected and desultory reading during his two years at Westminster, and even at this early date he began to concern himself with problems of chronology and historical criticism. 'The dynasties of Assyria and Egypt were my top and cricket-ball', he reminisced in later years, and he boasted, with considerable truth, that he 'arrived at Oxford with a stock of erudition that might have puzzled a Doctor, and a degree of ignorance of which a school boy would have been ashamed'.[3]

The mid-eighteenth century was not a brilliant period in Oxford's history, and in his later years Gibbon criticized the university unmercifully. Many of his contemporaries were equally critical, but we need not pause to enumerate their charges. We will merely point out that Gibbon's more abusive phrases — 'the monks of Magdalen', 'the bigots of Oxford', 'steeped in port and prejudice', 'their dull and deep potations' — betray a bitterness that did not spring wholly from a disinterested love of the truth. Such acrimony is evidence that he had once felt a deep emotional attachment to Oxford, but that this initial enthusiasm had been followed by unhappiness and disillusionment. In fact Gibbon tells us so himself. 'At the distance of forty years', he wrote in his Memoirs,[4] 'I still remember my first emotions of surprize and satisfaction', but fourteen months later he left the university for ever, and after forty years he could declare that 'she [Oxford] will as chearfully renounce me for a son as I am willing to disclaim her for a mother'. What caused this bitter disillusionment? To answer this question we must consider what the youthful Gibbon had expected Oxford to give him, what his father wished her to give, and what she was prepared to give.

Shortly after Gibbon's death in 1794 a correspondent signing himself simply 'D. P.' wrote to the *Gentleman's Magazine*,[5] 'I was Mr. Gibbon's bookseller at Oxford. He was a singular character, and but little connected with the young gentlemen of the College. They admit at Magdalen only men of fortune; no commoners.' These three lines explain much. Again the father had selected a college because of the social advantages it might confer upon his son, and Magdalen undertook to give the son an education appropriate to an eighteenth-century Englishman of fortune. Gibbon's awkwardness and shyness prevented him from taking advantage of his social opportunities, and his fellow students were disposed to laugh at his oddities. He therefore kept as far away from them as possible, taking refuge in the college library. Here he read widely, though he received little encouragement or guidance from his college.

Gibbon's first tutor at Oxford was a Dr. Thomas Waldegrave, a learned and kindly clergyman who took an interest in his pupil and won his confidence. But as long experience had taught the doctor that young gentlemen did not come to Magdalen to be made into scholars, he never assigned his pupils any serious tasks. In his Memoirs Gibbon took his tutor severely to task for this neglect, complaining that a perfunctory reading of three or four Latin plays was all that he got from Oxford.[6] On the same page, however, he tells of his many evening walks with his tutor, during which they conversed freely upon all manner of subjects. More than six years after leaving Oxford, Gibbon wrote him a friendly letter, now lost, and by return post he received a cordial reply beginning, 'I have read nothing for some time that has given me so much pleasure as your letter', and expressing a hope that his former pupil might visit him.[7] Though his old tutor was then rector of the parish church at Washington, a Sussex village barely twenty miles from

Buriton, Gibbon did not accept the invitation. Unfortunately Dr. Waldegrave left Oxford at the close of Gibbon's first term there, and his successor is known to history largely by his most famous pupil's famous quip, 'Dr. Winchester well remembered that he had a salary to receive, and only forgot that he had a duty to perform.'

Gibbon spoke with great exaggeration, however, when he asserted that his time at Oxford was wholly wasted. His mind was very active during those fourteen months, and he learned more at Magdalen than he later chose to admit. His Memoirs contain formidable lists of books which he claims to have studied before entering Oxford. It is well to remember, however, that Gibbon reached Oxford barely twenty months after leaving Westminster. More than half of this time he had spent as an invalid at Bath (where works of high scholarship would scarcely be available in the circulating libraries he patronized); another four months were passed in the house of a physician at Winchester; he was with an unsatisfactory tutor for a few weeks; and he spent much time travelling around England with his father. He undoubtedly read — or at least examined — many books during these twenty months, including works on history and chronology as well as books of travel and fiction, and quite possibly he tried to harmonize conflicting chronological tables, but it is difficult to believe that he read deeply in such difficult technical works as some of those he mentions. When Gibbon wrote this account of his early reading, forty years after the event, he was relying entirely upon his memory, and we may suspect that at times this memory deceived him. Later in his Memoirs, he himself suggests a more plausible source of his early erudition. When describing his first enthusiasm for Magdalen he reports that 'a key was delivered into my hands which gave me the free use of a numerous and learned library'.[8] It was doubtless in this library that Gibbon first stumbled upon most of the ponderous tomes he mentions, and it was there that by his own unaided efforts he discovered the delights of scholarship.

While at Oxford Gibbon plunged deeply into those Oriental

studies that had begun with his childhood reading of the *Arabian Nights* and had been continued in his grandfather Porten's library. 'Before I was sixteen' (that is, before he left Oxford), 'I had exhausted all that could be learned in English of the Arabs and Persians, the Tartars and Turks; and the same ardour urged me to guess at the French of d'Herbelot, and to construe the barbarous Latin of Pocock's Abulpharagius.' His Oxford bookseller (the 'D.P.' quoted above) recalled selling him a copy of d'Herbelot's *Bibliothèque orientale* (an encyclopedia of the Orient), and Gibbon tells us that he once confided to Dr. Waldegrave that he wished to learn Arabic. The tutor discouraged so unusual a project, but, undismayed by this cautious advice, Gibbon spent his first long vacation (1752) planning and writing a few pages of a book to be entitled *The Age of Sesostris*, a chronological study in which he tried to show that this Egyptian king was a contemporary of the Hebrew Solomon.[9]

During his first term at Magdalen Gibbon was not unhappy, but he made no close friends, and in his second term he began to be bored by his solitary studies. Seeking new diversions, he discovered that he could absent himself from Oxford for several days at a time with impunity, and he sought relief from boredom in travel. Having plenty of pocket money, he visited Bath and Buckinghamshire, and he made four trips to London, each lasting a week or more. These excursions gave him little pleasure, however, and again he took to desultory reading. A fellow student then lent him some books about the Catholic Church and, as Gibbon put it: 'At the age of sixteen I bewildered myself in the errors of the Church of Rome.'[10]

We may postpone our discussion of Gibbon's religious development to another chapter, but we must record here that on 8 June 1753 he was formally admitted to the Roman Catholic Church by a Jesuit attached to the Sardinian Embassy in London. The consequences of this conversion were immediate and overwhelming. The gates of Oxford were for ever closed against him, but as he made no attempt to return to the university the authorities there took no formal action against him. Gibbon's father was more deeply concerned. In fact the poor man was quite beside himself. The boy's rash act, if persisted in, would render for ever impossible the brilliant social and political career that his fond father was already planning for him. Hurrying from Buriton to London, the father took his truant son to Putney and consulted friends as to what should be done with him. One of these friends — Edward Eliot, a wealthy landowner and politician of Cornwall who was soon to marry Gibbon's cousin and who, on two later occasions, was destined to play a crucial part in the historian's career — suggested that the boy be sent for re-education to Lausanne in Switzerland. This suggestion was accepted; a reliable travelling companion was found; and on 19 June — just eleven days after his formal conversion — young Edward Gibbon entered upon a five-year exile from England.

These early experiences shaped Gibbon's whole life. While still a child he had absorbed something of his parents' admiration and awe for high society, but like them he never succeeded in forcing his way into the inner sanctum of that charmed world. His social failure sprang in considerable measure from his childhood misfortunes. Had it not been for his physical weakness and singularity, Westminster might have taught him to associate on equal terms with the sons of the social élite, and he might perhaps have made friends who would be willing and able to help him to enter their exalted sphere. His early illnesses were also the cause, no doubt, of his grotesque physical appearance in his mature years. Though slightly less than five feet tall he was enormously fat, and the ugliness of his face and figure were the occasion of many an unkind jest. He was often uncomfortable in society, and he sought to compensate for his physical defects by elaborate overdressing, vain ostentation, and ridiculous strutting. In fact these qualities became so deeply ingrained in his nature that they eventually dominated even his literary style. Had Gibbon's childhood been less unfortunate, his mature years would probably have been less troubled. But in that case he would not have written *The History of the Decline and Fall of the Roman Empire*.

During his five years at Lausanne Gibbon was under the care of a Calvinist clergyman, Daniel Pavillard, an intelligent and tactful man who soon won his pupil's respect and confidence. At first, however, the boy was unhappy in his new surroundings. In place of the elegant three-room apartment and servant which he had enjoyed at Oxford, his private domain now consisted of one small chamber, 'warmed by the dull invisible heat of a stove'; the food was poor, or at least not to his taste; the table linen was changed only once a week; Mme. Pavillard was 'ugly, dirty, proud, ill-natured, and covetous' (these are probably the unkindest words that Gibbon ever wrote, but she may have deserved them); he no longer had easy access to a library rich in scholarly books; and for a time his limited knowledge of French rendered him mute in society. He managed to find some Englishmen in Lausanne — including a few members of the aristocracy, as he carefully informed his father in his first letter home — but they soon proved to be undesirable companions. On one occasion, several months after his arrival in Lausanne, Gibbon lost over a hundred guineas to one of them at cards. He could not pay and, in a panic, he attempted to escape to England. He got as far as Geneva, forty miles away, before Pavillard found him and brought him back. By this time, however, Gibbon's immediate troubles were nearly over. He was learning to speak French; he was becoming habituated to Swiss ways; and he had made a place for himself in Swiss society at Lausanne. His remaining years at Lausanne were perhaps the happiest in his life, and ever thereafter he regarded Switzerland as a second fatherland.

Eighteen months after his arrival in Lausanne, Gibbon's reconversion was complete, and on Christmas Day 1754 he formally returned to Protestantism. The resolution of his religious difficulties was followed by a tremendous release of energy. Between the ages of eighteen and twenty-one he so perfected his French that he became bilingual; he read widely in French literature; he acquired a fluent reading knowledge of Latin and made a start in Greek; he carried his studies in mathematics through algebra and geometry; and he took a stiff course in logic. He set out to read the Latin authors from beginning to end and, according to the account he wrote many years later, he read over 3000 pages of Latin in 1755 and twice that amount in the following year. The foundations of Gibbon's massive learning were thus laid during these happy years at Lausanne, and in his Memoirs he stated quite truthfully that 'Whatsoever have been the fruits of my education, they must be ascribed to the fortunate shipwreck which cast me on the shores of the Leman lake.'[11]

At the same time Gibbon began to enjoy social life more than ever before. 'In the families of the first rank I was received with kindness and indulgence', he recalled when writing his Memoirs. 'My afternoons were filled by frequent and almost daily engagements to numerous or select parties of cards or conversation; and my choice of good company was the best preservative against the ignoble vices and follies of youth.' It happened, moreover, that during the winters of 1757 and 1758 the social life of Lausanne was enlivened and illuminated by the presence of the great Voltaire, who established his residence in the vicinity, staged his own tragedies in an improvised theatre, and played the *grand seigneur* generally. Gibbon attended several of his parties, but in later years he applied to himself Ovid's line, *Vergilium vidi tantum*, 'I only saw Virgil.' He was duly impressed, however, and, as he noted in his Memoirs, he 'then rated [Voltaire] above his real magnitude'.

During these last years at Lausanne Gibbon formed two lifelong friendships. A separate chapter must be reserved for his momentous love affair with Suzanne Curchod, later Madame Necker, but a paragraph will suffice for Georges Deyverdun. This young man belonged to a good Lausanne family, and though three years older than Gibbon he allowed the younger man to be his leader from the first. In his mature years Deyverdun cut no great figure in the world: he tutored the sons of English and German noblemen; he visited England and helped Gibbon in two early literary ventures; and he translated Goethe's *Werther* into French. But the suggestion that he take on the immense task of translating *The Decline and Fall* so appalled him that he could not even make a beginning. Gibbon and he remained firm friends for life, and the historian passed the last ten years of his life in Deyverdun's house at Lausanne.

When Gibbon left England in 1753 neither he nor his father had any idea as to how long his exile was to last. The father's immediate concern was to get his erring son back into the Protestant fold as quickly and quietly as possible, but he had no further plans for the boy's immediate future. Even after he had been informed that his son's reconversion was complete, and the boy was begging permission to come home, the father made no arrangements for his return to England. He apparently did not know what to do with his son and therefore did nothing. Perhaps bitter experience had by this time taught him that his strange son was not likely to profit from the conventional scholastic education of an English gentleman. At any rate, when Gibbon suggested that he return to England and complete his education at Cambridge, his father firmly vetoed the proposal. The father's conduct was also due in part to the fact that at just that time he was preparing to marry a Miss Dorothea Patton and was worried about his son's reaction to a second marriage. He tried to solve the problem by simply leaving the boy in Lausanne and saying nothing. At last, however, he wrote to his son early in January 1758 ordering him to come home, and speaking eloquently, though perhaps a trifle vaguely, of having great plans for his future.[12] As France and England were then at war, Gibbon's journey across France was rather hazardous, but he made it without incident and arrived in London on 5 May 1758.

It was with anxiety and trepidation that Gibbon looked forward to meeting his father and his new stepmother. Though the marriage had taken place in May 1755, his father had not mentioned it to him, either at the time or even in a 'vastly kind' letter dated 18 August. Some weeks later Gibbon learned the news from an incidental reference in a letter from a friend in Buriton. He wrote immediately to his Aunt Kitty to verify this disturbing report, but not until the following December, seven months after the event, did his father inform him of what had happened. Gibbon realized at once that his own future was deeply involved in this marriage. Should children be born to his father's second wife, they would of course inherit a share of their grandfather's fortune, and Gibbon wisely suspected that the residue of that fortune would not provide adequately for others beside himself. As it apparently had never occurred to him that he might earn a living by entering one of the professions, the prospect of rival heirs terrified him, and he approached his stepmother with a preconceived dislike. Everything turned out for the best, however, for the second Mrs. Gibbon bore no children, and she quickly won her stepson's lifelong esteem and affection. A few years later, after a visit with her, Gibbon confided to his Journal, 'I can't express the pleasure I had at seeing her. I love her as a companion, a friend, and a mother.'[13] A few months after her husband's death in 1770 Mrs. Gibbon wrote to a relative, 'I know that you will be glad to hear that Mr. Gibbon is most excessively kind and good to me. I think there never was a more worthy man.'[14] They retained this mutual esteem and affection throughout their lives, and Gibbon's letters to her are often franker and more revealing than those he wrote to his great friend Lord Sheffield.

It was not mere chance that fixed Gibbon's arrival in England on the eve of his twenty-first birthday. His father's finances had been deteriorating so rapidly of late that immediate and drastic action was necessary if he was to remain solvent. No money could be borrowed, however, until the entail on Gibbon's grandfather's estate was cut off, and Gibbon could not sign away his rights under the entail until he had reached the age of twenty-one. Soon after his birthday, however, he signed the necessary papers, and his father

Sheffield Place — the country house of Gibbon's best friend, John, Lord Sheffield. Gibbon often visited here

put a mortgage of £10,000 on the estate at Buriton. In return Gibbon was guaranteed an annuity of £300 for life.

Gibbon then established his residence in London, but though he took rooms in a fashionable district he made no friends of the sort that he and his father desired. His father's aristocratic acquaintances of ten years ago had forgotten him, or at least they were not now disposed to help his son, and Gibbon's few bashful efforts to revive acquaintanceships made at Westminster met with no success. His sole aid came from his father's old friend David Mallet, the minor poet at whose house in Putney Gibbon had passed the last ten days before his departure for Lausanne. Mallet did what he could to launch his friend's son on a social career, but his success was slight. He was himself a stranger to the better London society of the day, and Gibbon was not a very prepossessing protégé. The young man was therefore left pretty much to himself, and boredom again drove him to his books. Nevertheless an interesting entry in his Journal shows a slight social progress. This passage is worth quoting as evidence of his social ambition and his conception of the good life.

> I dined at the Cocoa tree. . . . That respectable body, of which I have the honour to be a member, affords every evening a sight truly English. Twenty or thirty, perhaps, of the first men in the kingdom, in point of fashion and fortune, supping at little tables covered with a napkin, in the middle of a Coffee-room, upon a bit of cold meat, or a Sandwich, & drinking a glass of punch. At present we are full of Privy Counsellors and Lords of the Bedchamber; who, having jumped into the Ministry, make a very singular medley of their old principles and language, with their modern ones.[15]

In those days a young man of Gibbon's tastes and social class could not maintain himself in London on £300 a year. It therefore became necessary for him to while away the summers as his father's guest at Buriton, after which he could afford to pass a few winter months as a young man of fortune in the city. Unfortunately, however, country life held few charms for Gibbon. As he seldom rode a horse and never handled a gun, he was quite content to stay at home, reading a book, while his father galloped over the countryside following the hounds of their neighbour, the Duke of Richmond. He came to dread the period of the full moon, he tells us, because inescapable social diversions were then prolonged far into the night, but he dutifully attended the near-by races, in which his father usually entered a horse. Gibbon later wrote that he even came to enjoy the spectacle. In other ways as well he gradually became habituated to his new life, and though he complained in his Journal about 'the contemptible character of a meer country squire', a casual observer would have seen little reason to suspect that this strange and lonely young man was not destined to become a country squire himself. After two years, however, this monotonous existence gave way to active service in the militia.

At the outbreak of the Seven Years War (1756–63) the British Army had been made up largely of mercenaries (many of them Germans) who were soon sent to fight on the Continent or to defend distant parts of the empire. When England was thus denuded of troops, fear of a French invasion arose, and people began demanding an armed force capable of coping with such an emergency. Parliament therefore passed a militia Act in 1757. A few recruits were enlisted and drilled, but not much was accomplished until two years later, when a second invasion scare led to greater activity. It was decreed that each county should provide one or more battalions of militia, with officers drawn from the gentry of that county. Gibbon and his father volunteered for service, the father being commissioned a major, the son a captain (12 June 1759).

At first the Gibbons believed their duties would be limited to drill on a few afternoons every month, but they were soon undeceived. Their battalion was called to the colours (10 May 1760) and remained in camp until December 1762. For two and a half years Gibbon drilled his company, marching it back and forth from one camp to another in southern England, but as there was no

French invasion he saw no actual fighting. At first he enjoyed drilling his men and took pride in his company; he saw aspects of life that were new to him; but he learned to drink heavily, and in general his character was coarsened. After a few months of this new life he remarked in his Journal: 'The charm was over, I was sick of so hateful a service, tired of companions who had neither the knowledge of scholars nor the manners of gentlemen.'[16] Thirty years later, when he came to write his Memoirs, Gibbon copied out the last half of this sentence (though Lord Sheffield suppressed it in his edition), but in the same passage he admitted that he had profited in many ways from his army experience. The militia had rubbed off some of his French mannerisms, making him 'an Englishman and a soldier'; it taught him something of military science; and he asserted that 'the Captain of the Hampshire grenadiers (the reader may smile) has not been useless to the historian of the Roman Empire'.

During the first seven or eight months of his 'military servitude' Gibbon found no time for reading or study, and he recorded in his Journal that 'I hardly took a book in my hand'. Early in 1761, however, he once more began to 'taste the pleasure of thinking', but before long he was interrupted again. Rumours of peace were beginning to circulate, and Gibbon's father devised a plan for securing the appointment of his son as secretary to one of the British diplomats at the impending peace conference. The plan was not a bad one. Shortly before leaving Lausanne young Gibbon had started to write a book, in French, on the advantages to be derived from studying ancient literature, but after completing a first draft at Buriton in February 1759 he laid the manuscript aside. Two years later the elder Gibbon had the happy idea that if his son could display his mastery of French by publishing a book in that language, he might be rewarded with a diplomatic appointment. A publisher was therefore found, and the *Essai sur l'étude de la littérature* appeared in July 1761. Gibbon's only payment consisted of forty copies of the book, twenty of which he sent to friends in Lausanne, while the others were presented to prominent Englishmen (selected by his father and Mallet) who were in a position to advance the young author's political and social career. The rumours of peace proved to be premature, however, and the elder Gibbon's scheme came to nothing.

Meantime Gibbon had made his own plans for the immediate future. When the war was over, and the militia had been demobilized (23 December 1762), he persuaded his father to allow him a two-year visit to Europe. He planned to pass several weeks in Paris, to spend the winter in Lausanne, and to travel in Italy in 1764. He left England on 25 January 1763 and reached Paris three days later.

When Gibbon arrived in Paris he was delighted to find that his fame had preceded him and that people in literary circles had heard of his *Essai*. In fact it had been reprinted in Paris in 1762, and it gave its author a standing in Paris as a man of letters. This was all very nice, but Gibbon was anxious to be accepted as a man of fashion as well. He therefore took an apartment in the aristocratic suburb of St.-Germain at six guineas a month; his coach cost him sixteen guineas more; and he felt obliged to purchase a large supply of expensive French clothes. Letters of introduction brought him invitations to a few fine houses, but his Journal betrays his chagrin at not receiving more. When the Duke of Bedford, British ambassador at Paris, could not be bothered to entertain the young stranger, Gibbon reported this negligence to his father and suggested that he complain to their neighbour, the Duke of Richmond, who had given him a letter to the 'great Duke'.

In spite of these disappointments Gibbon enjoyed himself immensely in Paris. He usually devoted his mornings to sightseeing, while his afternoons and evenings were spent in society. Not long after his arrival he reported to his stepmother, 'In a fortnight passed at Paris I have heard more conversation worth remembering, & seen more men of letters amongst the people of fashion, than I had done in two or three winters in London.' He met and dined with such *philosophes* as d'Alembert and Diderot, Helvétius and Holbach, and he felt flattered by their polite attentions. He also enjoyed meeting a few scholars whom he knew by reputation. But the chief attraction of Paris for him seems to have been a certain Madame Bontems, a middle-aged lady with literary interests who had translated Thomson's *Seasons* into French prose. She took an interest in the young Englishman; she accompanied him on visits to points of interest in or near the city; and he spent much of his time at her apartment. It was she rather than the scholars and *philosophes* who made his stay in Paris delightful.

Nearly thirty years later Gibbon declared, in his Memoirs, that if only he had been rich and independent he might have established a permanent residence in Paris. He may have remembered it that way, but at the time Switzerland seemed more attractive than Paris, and after fourteen weeks in the French capital he proceeded to Lausanne (May 1763).

Many old friends, including Pavillard, welcomed him warmly upon his arrival in Lausanne, but his second stay in that city differed notably from the first. He was no longer a boy under the care of a clergyman; he was a grown man, twenty-six years of age, free to come and go as he pleased. Taking quarters in a fashionable pension, he made the acquaintance of several wild young Englishmen whom he sometimes joined in their drinking sprees. On at least one occasion the revellers found themselves in trouble with the Lausanne police.[17] After an exceptionally discreditable affair on the night of 14 September Gibbon's conduct improved, but the damage had been done and his good name was tarnished. Thoroughly ashamed of himself, he wrote in his Journal, 'I once had a very fine reputation here for my moral character, but I notice that people are now beginning to identify me with my Compatriots and to consider me a man who loves wine and disorder. Are they completely mistaken?' He began to dislike Lausanne, and in the following April, shortly before he left the city, he confided to his Journal: 'I quit

Lausanne with less regret than on the first occasion. I leave behind only acquaintances.'[18]

In spite of these diversions and distractions Gibbon worked hard during his months at Lausanne. In preparation for his Italian tour he made a systematic study of the geography of ancient Italy, and he did a tremendous amount of general reading, especially in the *Bibliothèque raisonnée* — a periodical published in Holland, which gave reviews, abstracts, and long excerpts from contemporary works of literature and scholarship. In the course of the winter Gibbon worked his way through its fifty volumes (1728–53), finding in each three or four or more articles which he read and mentioned in his Journal. The mere keeping of this Journal was a feat in itself. In its 270 pages he chronicled his social activities, summarized his reading, and wrote several long criticisms of what he had read. It might seem that such labours would satisfy the severest taskmaster, yet we find Gibbon frequently complaining in his Journal of days lost and of his own laziness.

It was during this second visit to Lausanne that Gibbon began his lifelong friendship with John Holroyd, later Lord Sheffield. Holroyd reached Lausanne soon after Gibbon's arrival, and the two men at once became fast friends. They differed so greatly from each other in character and pursuits that in later years Gibbon sometimes wondered why they were drawn to each other, but for thirty years Holroyd remained his closest friend. Gibbon was a frequent and welcome visitor at Sheffield Place (Holroyd's estate in Sussex some fifty miles south of London), and for many years Gibbon allowed his friend to manage his business affairs. But Sheffield's greatest service to Gibbon was his edition of the historian's Memoirs and other papers, which added so greatly to his reputation.*

* Gibbon's biographers often picture Holroyd as a rather colourless figure whose sole claim to fame derived from his friendship with Gibbon — as a Dr. Watson, perhaps, to a Sherlock Holmes. Nothing could be farther from the truth. Holroyd was an important person in his own right. Descended from a Yorkshire family which had acquired large holdings in Ireland under Charles II, Holroyd sat in the House of Commons for Coventry in 1780 and again from

On 18 April 1764 Gibbon set out for Italy, accompanied by William Guise,[19] a young Englishman whom he had met in Lausanne. They crossed the Alps by the Mont Cenis pass, proceeded through northern Italy in a leisurely fashion, and spent three months in Florence. Here they studied Italian (a language Gibbon never became proficient in), visited museums and art galleries, and took part in the social activities of the English colony. Not until late in September did they resume their journey, but at long last, on the evening of 2 October 1764, they entered Rome.

Gibbon was in a state of high excitement during his first days in Rome.[20] 'I am really almost in a dream', he wrote to his father a week after his arrival, and in his Memoirs he declared that 'at the distance of twenty-five years I can neither forget nor express the strong emotions which agitated my mind as I first approached and entered the *eternal City*. After a sleepless night, I trod with lofty step the ruins of the Forum; each memorable spot where Romulus *stood*, or Tully spoke, or Caesar fell, was at once present to my eye; and several days of intoxication were lost or enjoyed before I could descend to a cool and minute investigation.' Unfortunately, however, we can no longer trace his activities or the progress of his thoughts day by day, for in his excitement he found no time to write in his Journal: its last entry is dated 2 October.

1781 to 1784, and for Bristol from 1790 to 1802, staunchly supporting Lord North during the American Revolution and opposing the younger Pitt during the early years of his ministry. In 1780 he became a baron in the Irish peerage; in 1802 he entered the House of Lords as a baron of the English peerage; and in 1816 he was created an English earl. He was much interested in the new scientific agriculture, carrying on an extensive correspondence with Arthur Young, making Sheffield Place one of the model farms of England, and finally becoming president of the Board of Agriculture (1803). He was also a fellow of the Royal Society. He wrote important tracts on various economic problems: American commerce (1783), Ireland (1784), in defence of the slave trade (1790) and the Corn Laws (1791 and 1815). He was a convinced mercantilist, and was praised by his friend Gibbon as the saviour of the Navigation Act, 'the palladium of Britain'. Though two years older than Gibbon, Holroyd survived him by more than a quarter of a century, and died in 1821. The biography he deserves is yet to be written.

After spending eighteen weeks in Rome and six in Naples, Gibbon and Guise began their homeward journey. Passing through Bologna and Loretto, they visited Venice briefly in mid-April, crossed the Alps by the Mont Cenis pass once more, and arrived in Lyons at the end of May. They had intended to spend about six weeks travelling in southern France and then sail from Bordeaux to England, but his father's financial difficulties forced Gibbon to give up this excursion. Guise went south alone and Gibbon proceeded to Paris. After stopping there for two weeks he reached London late in June 1765. He had been abroad for two years and a half.

The next several years were not happy ones for Gibbon, and in his Memoirs he sadly records that they were the portion of his life which he passed with the least enjoyment and remembered with the least satisfaction.[21] 'While so many of my acquaintance were married or in parliament, or advancing with a rapid step in the various roads of honour and fortune, I stood alone, immoveable and insignificant; . . . I lamented that at the proper age I had not embraced the lucrative pursuits of the law or of trade, the chances of civil office or India adventure, or even the fat slumbers of the Church . . .'[22] Indeed, it seemed that Gibbon was destined to pass his life as a 'meer country squire', — a fate he found it hard to reconcile himself to.

As his father's health was failing (the poor man eventually became blind), it devolved upon the son to manage the estate and to bring some sort of order into the family finances. With his stepmother's aid the Buriton property was made profitable, but the second task was impossible and Gibbon never mastered it.

The elder Gibbon died in November 1770, thus closing a pathetic life. He had failed in everything important that he ever undertook. He was deeply devoted to his first wife, and tried to give her the social life she so ardently craved, but she died when he was only forty, and he was helpless without her. There can be no doubt that he was deeply attached to his son, or that his son was equally fond of him, but the two men simply could not understand each other. The father wanted his son to have the best, which in his opinion meant sitting in Parliament and mixing socially with the 'best' people — that is, the most aristocratic and wealthy. Gibbon was not insensitive to the charms of such a life; he really wanted the things his father wanted him to have; but there were other things that he wanted even more, and in the end his father usually indulged him. The father could ill afford his son's second trip to the Continent, for example, yet he provided the money when his son asked for it. Gibbon was a difficult son for a country squire of limited means, and his biographers rarely give his father the credit he merits.

As his father died intestate Gibbon had to spend many weary months straightening out his affairs, and not until two years later was the task completed. The house at Putney had already been sold (1769); Buriton was now leased to a tenant; the father's more pressing debts were paid; and Gibbon was made 'exquisitely happy at feeling so many Mountains taken off my shoulders'. Mrs. Gibbon went to live at Bath, with an annuity of £200 plus £100 interest on a note she held, and late in 1772 Gibbon took up his residence in London. His *Wanderjahre* were over and a new period in his life began.

Gibbon, now thirty-five years old, was impatient to establish himself in London as a gentleman and a scholar. He therefore rented a rather impressive house in Bentinck Street, near Portman Place and not far from Kensington Gardens. Here he lived in style, keeping six servants and a carriage, and here he wrote the first four volumes of *The Decline and Fall.* The next ten years (1773–83) were the busiest of his life. His various social and political activities usually occupied his afternoons and evenings, but his mornings were reserved for his primary occupation, which was writing his History. It was during these busy years that he composed that History's most famous chapters.

Gibbon often boasted in his Memoirs of his distinguished friends in London's literary and political worlds. One group of these friends centred around the famous Literary Club, which had been founded in 1765 by Sir Joshua Reynolds and to which Gibbon was elected in 1774. This club is now known chiefly from Boswell's *Life of Johnson*, where Johnson is glorified while Gibbon receives very unfair treatment. He is pictured as fearing Johnson and as replying to his attacks only by muttering under his breath. As a matter of fact Gibbon probably played almost as important a role in the club as Johnson himself. The records show that he attended 88 club dinners, being second only to Reynolds, who attended 152 during the same years, while Johnson was present at only 31 and Boswell at 27.[23] Gibbon was on friendly terms with such other members of the club as R. B. Sheridan, the dramatist and parliamentary orator; and Garrick, the actor; William Jones, the Orientalist, who was the first to emphasize the similarities of Sanskrit with Greek and Latin; and, above all, the economist Adam Smith. Smith's *Wealth of Nations* was published by the same publisher and in the same year as the first volume of *The Decline and Fall* (1776), and by a Will dated in 1788 Gibbon left Smith 100 guineas 'to remind him of a departed friend'. Smith died in 1790, however, so this bequest was stricken from Gibbon's final will, drawn up in 1792.

The most distinguished socially of Gibbon's literary friends was not a member of the club. This was Horace Walpole, son of the prime minister who had ruined Gibbon's grandfather and whom Gibbon's father had helped to vote out of office. At first Walpole only laughed at Gibbon, calling him 'the son of a foolish alderman', but he was among the first to recognize the merits of *The Decline and Fall.* Gibbon put Walpole down as an elegant trifler, but though Walpole often held him up to ridicule Gibbon continued to attend his receptions. Some of Gibbon's political friends were also members of the club, notably Burke and Charles James Fox. Regarding the latter, Gibbon wrote to Madame Necker, 'He is one of the most extraordinary men of his time. Je l'admire, je le plains, et je l'aime.' In his later years, however, Gibbon was more attracted to Wedderburn, the attorney-general who presently became lord chancellor, and Lord North, the prime minister to whom he dedicated the last three volumes of his History.

Gibbon thus achieved fame and made his way into London society, but we may suspect that his triumphs were not quite so spectacular as he would like to have us believe. At any rate he was far from happy during these years. When with intimate friends he was a brilliant conversationalist, though he insisted on being the leader and brooked no contradiction. Before strangers, however, he was apt to be ill at ease and somewhat obsequious, partly perhaps because wits were constantly holding him up to ridicule — not always behind his back. His parliamentary career ended in disaster, and he found to his sorrow that the remnants of his grandfather's fortune could not support him in the style to which he aspired. And finally he discovered that his only true friends in England were his Aunt Kitty, his stepmother, and the Holroyds — now Lord and Lady Sheffield. His imagination carried him back to the happy days of his youth at Lausanne, and in spite of the protests of these friends, he packed up his books and moved to Lausanne in September 1783 — aged forty-six years. It is interesting to note that his father, when at about that age, had similarly admitted defeat and withdrawn from London society to become a country squire, but that his grandfather, having lost most of his fortune at that same age, persevered and erected a new fortune on the ruins of the old.

One of Lausanne's chief attractions for Gibbon was the friend of his youth, Georges Deyverdun. The two men had not seen each other for several years, but they had never forgotten their old friendship. Gibbon therefore rented half of Deyverdun's house in Lausanne, and the two men lived happily together until Deyverdun's death in 1789. From him Gibbon inherited a life interest in the house, where he continued to live until his death nearly five years later.

Gibbon insisted to his stepmother and the Sheffields that he had no regrets for having left London and that he was never happier than during his last years at Lausanne. The frequency of his self-justifications may arouse our suspicions, but his statements undoubtedly were true. He was very happy in his new home. His friend E. T. Langer (the man who gave him a copy of John Gibbon's book on heraldry) tells us that when he first met Gibbon in London, in 1782, the historian had been stiff and unapproachable, but when they met again at Lausanne two years later he was very sociable and at ease.[24] Gibbon was well received in Lausanne society, and the strain under which he had lived during his last years in London was over. He was Lausanne's most distinguished citizen, and socially he was 'King of the Place'.* He had finally achieved recognition as a man of letters *and* a man of fashion, as a gentleman *and* a scholar.

Gibbon's ten years at Lausanne may be summarized very briefly. He finished the last two volumes of his History and returned to London in 1787 to see them through the press. Within a year, however, he was back in Lausanne, revolving in his mind various literary projects, which eventually came to nothing, and composing the six drafts of his Memoirs. Then came word of Lady Sheffield's death (April 1793), and Gibbon hurried back to England to comfort his bereaved friend. He had every intention of returning to Lausanne, but he died suddenly and unexpectedly in London on 16 January 1794, aged fifty-six years. A week later his coffin was placed in Lord Sheffield's family vault, which fills the north transept of the parish church at Fletching, a village some three miles from Sheffield Place.

* Maria Josepha Holroyd, Lord Sheffield's vivacious and keen-eyed daughter, made some interesting remarks about Gibbon in letters to her aunt written during her family's visit to Lausanne in 1791: 'I own my surprise is very great that Mr. Gibbon should chuse to spend his days here in preference to England, for there does not appear to me to be anybody with whom he can converse on equal terms, or who is worthy to hear him; but it is a proof how much pleasure Flattery gives the most intelligent people. This is the only advantage this place can have over England for him. . . . Mr. Gibbon dislikes the French very much, which is nothing but Swiss prejudice, of which he has imbibed a large quantity. . . . When the "King of the Place," as he is called, opens his mouth, (which, you know he generally does some time before he has arranged his sentence), all wait in awful and respectful silence for what shall follow, and look up to it as an Oracle.' (J. Adeane, *The Girlhood of Maria Josepha Holroyd*, 63, 73, 77.)

CHAPTER THREE

GIBBON AS A LOVER

WHEN Gibbon left England at the age of sixteen, he had never associated with girls of his own age, and during his first years in Switzerland he fared no better. Eventually, however, his developing social talents enabled him to make friends of both sexes, and the young people of the better families in Lausanne accepted the well-to-do young Englishman as a member of their set. The most important of his new feminine friends formed a group called 'la Société du Printemps', whose fifteen or twenty members met regularly at each other's houses, where they were permitted to entertain young men without chaperonage. 'They laughed, they sung, they danced, they played at cards, they acted comedies; but in the midst of this careless gayety they respected themselves, and were respected by the men.' Holroyd's early letters corroborate Gibbon's account of the Printemps. He wrote that he attended its assemblies 'most devoutly' every Sunday, and he observed that in Switzerland young ladies 'are not so reserved as English misses, but are extremely shy of pawing and handling'.[1] Holroyd's reports come from the period of Gibbon's second stay in Lausanne, it is true, but conditions had changed very little during the five intervening years, and it was in this atmosphere that Gibbon fell in love for the first and only time in his life.

The lady who inspired this love was Mademoiselle Suzanne Curchod. Barely a month younger than Gibbon, Suzanne was the only child of the pastor at Crassy — now Crassier — a village some fifteen miles north of Geneva and a few miles off the main road to Lausanne. In June 1757 she visited relatives in Lausanne, where her beauty, wit, vivacity, and high intelligence quickly attracted favourable attention. At just this time Gibbon happened to be suffering from a severe attack of homesickness and had recently written his father a despondent letter, complaining of being forced to live among foreigners for four years and begging permission to come home. Then he began to hear glowing reports of the brilliant and charming Mlle. Curchod, he met her, and, as he succinctly put it, 'I saw and loved.'[2]

Suzanne received his attentions gladly. Early in August she invited him to Crassy for two days, and a little later he spent a month in Geneva, where she, too, was visiting. When returning to Lausanne, he went out of his way to pass through Crassy, and a few days later he wrote his first letter to Suzanne. It was a turbulent composition, bantering in style and expressing all the sentiments that are expected of a romantic lover. He praised her charms; he reported that exactly 121 hours, 18 minutes, and 33 seconds had passed since the beginning of his 'exile'; he compared himself to Adam expelled from the Garden; and he remarked that his conduct since his return to Lausanne had made everyone there consider him insane — but he neglected to mention a six-page letter (in Latin), dealing with matters of high scholarship, which he had sent on the preceding day to a professor in Zürich. Despite his tempestuous professions of undying love, Gibbon carefully kept first things first: scholarship took precedence, and the lady had to wait.*

* The exact date of Gibbon's letter to Suzanne (*Letters*, I, 68–71) is important because of the light it throws upon his character as a lover and the depth of his feeling for Suzanne. The letter bears no date, but by complicated calculations the editors plausibly assign it to 19 October 1757. Gibbon's six-page letter to Professor J. J. Breitinger, of Zürich, is dated 18 October (*Letters*, I, 58–64). This erudite and carefully prepared epistle, which contains 35 references to 18 ancient authors and names 15 modern scholars, obviously was not written in a hurry. Gibbon probably had planned it before he went to Geneva, and may even have composed a first draft, but as the letter mentions his recent trip to Geneva, he must have prepared the final draft after his return. We should allow him at least a day or two to put the letter into its final form. Whatever may be the date of Gibbon's letter to Suzanne, it certainly was written after the one to Breitinger. We may also remark that, if composing this Latin letter was Gibbon's

Suzanne answered his letter on the twenty-fourth, using the same gay and bantering style that he had assumed. While they were at Geneva she had told him of an impending visit to friends in Rolle, and they had agreed to a rendezvous there. Her mother disapproved of this plan, however, and in her letter Suzanne begged Gibbon 'most seriously' not to come. When thus forced to give up his visit to Rolle, Gibbon decided to call instead upon an acquaintance at Luins (a village a few miles beyond Rolle), and he saw Suzanne briefly as he drove through the town (1 November).[3] A fortnight later she invited him to visit her at Crassy again, and he spent six days at her home (17–23 November). During this third visit to Crassy Gibbon asked Suzanne to marry him. According to her account of the episode (written five years later, when under great emotional stress) she wished to show him that she was not influenced by his money and therefore told him of the proposal of a certain M. de Montplaisir — a wealthy but rather dull Swiss who had been courting her for some time. Much to her surprise (she asserted) Gibbon replied by proposing to her himself. She avoided giving him a direct answer, but she told him quite positively that she could never leave her elderly parents alone in Switzerland.[4] Gibbon accepted this condition and returned to his books in Lausanne.

A week or so later, about 1 December, Gibbon sent Suzanne a second letter, to which she replied promptly. Her reply has been lost, but in his third letter, written towards the end of the month, Gibbon reported to her that he had read it through 'forty-two' times. Suzanne replied on 10 January, writing in the same gay spirit as before, but in none of these letters did either party refer to marriage or even to Gibbon's proposal. Three weeks passed, and Suzanne received no reply to her letter. Wounded in her pride, and worried a little perhaps by a fear that his love for her had cooled

---

chief occupation during the first few days after his return from Geneva, there is some question as to the accuracy of his statement that everyone in Lausanne considered him *fou* — unless, of course, we are willing to concede that any ambitious young scholar who works hard must be crazy.

during the three months she had kept him dangling, she wrote him again early in February, reproaching him for his neglect. Her letter has been lost, but according to Gibbon's reply, date 9 February, she treated him as though he were 'the basest of men'; she accused him of deserting her; and she even suggested that he might declare himself indifferent to her. Gibbon heatedly assured her of his undying love and fidelity, and explained that he and a few friends had gone on a brief excursion to Fribourg and Berne, where they had been detained longer than he had anticipated. He said that they had left Lausanne on 4 January and had not returned until 3 February. Though Gibbon certainly took no such trip,* Suzanne accepted his excuses and pressed the matter no further, for by this time more important difficulties had arisen.

Why had Gibbon neglected to answer Suzanne's letter, and why did he concoct this cock-and-bull story to explain his neglect? The reason is not far to seek. At just this time — early January 1758 — Gibbon received a letter from his father calling him back to England. The letter has been lost, but we know its general purport from Gibbon's account of it to Suzanne. Gibbon saw a storm brewing. His father's references to a brilliant career being prepared for him (probably with an immediate seat in Parliament) opened the son's eyes to the likelihood of strong parental opposition to his marrying and settling in Switzerland. In his letter of 9 February Gibbon tactlessly admitted to Suzanne that he had anticipated

* There are several reasons for doubting the truth of Gibbon's statement. He had told Suzanne nothing of the proposed trip in his third letter, written shortly before 4 January, and he makes no reference to it in his Journal, though all his other trips in Switzerland are duly recorded there. Moreover, Gibbon stated in his Journal that on 23 January he saw Voltaire act in *Alzire* at Lausanne. (This date, recorded from memory more than three years later, may not be exact, but there can be little doubt that Gibbon saw the play some time in January.) More important than this contradiction, however, are two documents published in Gibbon's *Miscellaneous Works*, III, 150–1 and 152–69. One is a comparative chronological table, the other a detailed essay on ancient chronology. Each is dated at Lausanne, with the table clearly marked 'January 13, 1758', and the essay dated ten days later. Gibbon obviously was in Lausanne at the time when he claimed to have been in Fribourg and Berne.

trouble with his father because she had no dowry, and he now declared that he foresaw trouble because his father would expect him to live in England. He promised Suzanne that he would do what he could to win his parent's consent to their marriage, and though he bombastically declared that 'l'amour me rendra éloquent', he obviously had little hope of success. He already was prepared to obey his father.

Gibbon's letter evoked a passionate reply. Suzanne took her revenge for the reference to her poverty by remarking that when he did not answer her letter she assumed that of course it was because he had found some other woman who had more money than she, and after complimenting him sarcastically upon his tender concern for his father, she told him that she had devised a plan which should satisfy both their parents. She then invited him to come to Crassy and discuss plans for their future.[5]

Early in March Gibbon made his fourth and final visit to Crassy. We have no record of what he and Suzanne said to each other, but it seems clear that she finally promised to marry him. They would be married soon, but after their marriage he would live in England and she in Switzerland until their parents died. They would limit themselves to visiting each other for two or three months in alternate years. Suzanne's plan was fantastic, but Gibbon agreed to it. When he left Crassy on 5 March he and Suzanne considered themselves engaged, and she had evidently become deeply attached to him. There are no letters from either of the lovers written during the remaining month of Gibbon's stay in Lausanne, which seems rather strange, but we have one pertinent document which is not exactly a letter. Gibbon's Journal informs us that three days after his return to Lausanne he wrote the opening pages of the book that he eventually published under the title, *Essai sur l'étude de la littérature.* He undoubtedly had discussed his plans for such a book with Suzanne, and apparently he promised to dedicate it to her. The document in question is a flowery 'Epître Dedicatoire', obviously written while he still was in Lausanne.[6] It is our last document dating from the idyllic period of Gibbon's romance, and it did not appear in the *Essai* when that little book was published three years later.

During the ten months of his love affair at Lausanne, Gibbon had not once mentioned Suzanne in his letters to his family. This silence is easily understood. Gibbon respected, loved, and feared his father, and he had been frightened by the unannounced addition of a stepmother to the family. He was therefore careful always to express himself as the most subservient and dutiful of sons. Moreover he foresaw that his father would object strenuously to receiving a daughter-in-law who had neither fortune nor social position — and who was a foreigner besides. During the first weeks following his return to England both he and his father were so busy arranging the mortgage on the Buriton estate that he considered the time inopportune for discussions of so delicate a matter as matrimony. Only after they had been at Buriton for several weeks did he find the courage to ask his father's permission to marry Suzanne. The father immediately and indignantly refused to countenance such a match. 'Go marry your foreigner, you are independent', his son quoted him as saying, 'but before you go, remember that you are a son and a citizen.' Gibbon withdrew to his room, where he meditated for two hours, and then returned to tell his father that 'I sacrificed to him all the happiness of my life'. In his Memoirs Gibbon summarized his surrender in the famous phrase, 'I sighed as a lover, I obeyed as a son', but there was more to it than that — much more.[7]

We do not know the exact date of Gibbon's conversation with his father, but we have the letter, dated 24 August 1758, in which he informed Suzanne of what had happened and told her that he must break off their engagement. She replied with a hysterical letter, dated 7 September, in which, among other things, she reproached him for having decided to relinquish her after only two hours of meditation. Gibbon's critics have often repeated this reproach. As a matter of fact, however, Gibbon had long since decided that he would give up Suzanne if his father refused to sanction the marriage. This decision was due in part, no doubt, to Gibbon's strong family feeling and his affection for his father, but actually there was nothing he could do except bow to his father's will. Gibbon was now twenty-one years of age; he had been brought up as a man of leisure; his greatest desire was to lead a life of study; he had no money of his own except an annuity of £300; and he had no skills that might enable him to supplement this scanty income. Though the angry father might say to the son, 'You are independent', they both knew very well that as long as the father lived the son would be dependent upon his bounty. 'Without his consent I was myself destitute and helpless', Gibbon wrote truthfully in his Memoirs. Gibbon and Suzanne had been indulging in romantic dreams of love and marriage, and, like many romantic lovers, they had paid little attention to the hard facts of life. When they were finally forced to learn these facts in bitter sorrow, Gibbon learned them better and more quickly than Suzanne.

Suzanne's letter of 7 September did not reach Gibbon until several months later. His stepmother had intercepted it and had written to Suzanne, reporting what had happened to the letter, warning her that the same fate would overtake any others that she might send, and advising her to forget Gibbon and marry somebody else. Suzanne wrote to Gibbon at once (5 November), informing him of what his stepmother had done, but as she dared not entrust this second letter to the post, she gave it to a Genevan acquaintance who was going to London and asked him to deliver it to Gibbon personally. Gibbon did not receive the letter until the following February.

Gibbon had by this time settled in London for the winter, but immediately upon receiving Suzanne's letter he hurried to Buriton, where he had a stormy session with his father. His father remained obdurate, but his stepmother gave him the letter she had intercepted. Gibbon was so annoyed that he wrote Suzanne a long letter from London (23 February) describing the scene with his father, speaking bitterly of parents in general, and assuring her, in terms as strong as any that he had used in Switzerland, that she was the only woman who could ever make him happy and that his love for her would never die. Even when in this exalted state, however, Gibbon did not forget that marriage to Suzanne was out of the question. He told her that they must 'yield to necessity', and he advised her not to write to him again — though he gave her a London address to which she could safely send letters. It is hard to read this letter and doubt that Gibbon still loved Suzanne. He had been making great efforts to reconcile himself to the inevitable, but for the moment his self-imposed discipline broke down and he poured out his true feeling. His letter naturally encouraged her to continue hoping, and she presently wrote him once more, urging that at least they could exchange four letters a year. By this time, however, Gibbon had regained control of himself, and he did not reply to her letter.

A few weeks later Gibbon entered the militia (June 1759), and though his battalion was not mobilized until May 1760, he was occupied all summer with militia business. After another year had passed, he began keeping a journal (24 August 1761), filling in the important events of his earlier life briefly and as best he could remember them. A curious entry shows how his feelings about Suzanne had changed during these two years. Recording their first meeting at Lausanne he wrote: 'June [1757]. I saw Mademoiselle Curchod, omnia vincit amor et nos cedamus amori.'[8] Most commentators see only the last half of Virgil's line and assume that this quotation was merely Gibbon's way of saying that he and Suzanne fell in love with each other. It seems more probable, however, that the first three words of the quotation were, in Gibbon's mind, its most important part. He was reminding himself that in 1757 he had fondly believed that love conquers all, though he later learned to his sorrow that it does not. Gibbon was in love no longer, but he already showed a fondness for irony.

The summer of 1758 had been a pleasant one for Suzanne. She was twenty-one years old, engaged to a brilliant and wealthy young man, and quite sure that he would soon come back to Switzerland and marry her. In this happy frame of mind she spent July visiting friends in Lausanne, where she again enjoyed great social success. Then, soon after her return to Crassy, came the crushing news from England. Suzanne was not a woman to give up without a struggle, however, and during the next few months she frantically tried to save something from the wreckage — even if it was only the exchange of four letters a year. Early in 1760 her father died, and as she now admitted the hopelessness of her dreams about Gibbon, she consented to marry M. de Montplaisir. At the last moment, however, she refused to go through with the marriage. She was thus reduced to supporting her mother and herself as a governess in Geneva, where she was widely admired for her high character, her courage, and her devotion to her mother. But she was an ambitious woman to whom her present position was intolerable. When her mother died, in January 1763, Suzanne began planning to leave Geneva. Such was her state of mind when she heard, in May, that Gibbon was in Lausanne.

During the next week Suzanne wrote him two letters, inquiring about his feeling for her and soliciting his friendship. When Gibbon replied, three weeks later, he began by exclaiming, 'Must you always offer me a happiness which my reason obliges me to renounce?' after which he accepted her friendship but declined further correspondence.* Things took a turn for the worse in August, when

* Suzanne even tried to persuade the great Jean-Jacques Rousseau to intervene with Gibbon in her behalf. She had read *La Nouvelle Héloïse* soon after its publication in 1761, and in it she may have seen her own story with parts reversed. (In Rousseau's romance a rich heiress and a poor tutor fall in love, but her parents refuse to let them marry.) In 1763 Rousseau was living in Switzerland, near Neuchâtel, and in May of that year, just as Gibbon was arriving in Lausanne, Suzanne's employer (a Genevese clergyman named Moultou) was visiting him. Moultou told Suzanne's sad story to Rousseau and asked him to speak to Gibbon about her. Rousseau refused, saying that 'whoever does not realize her value is not worthy of her, but he who has known it and can break off is a man to despise'. Several years later, after Rousseau's death, this letter was published. Gibbon saw it and added a footnote to his Memoirs: 'As an author I shall not appeal from the judgement, or taste, or caprice of

Gibbon went to Ferney to see Voltaire act the part of Genghis Khan in his tragedy *L'Orphelin de la Chine*. Suzanne was there too; they exchanged bitter words; and a few weeks later (21 September) she sent him a long and passionate letter in which she recounted the whole story of their love affair. Gibbon noted the receipt of this letter in his Journal, called her a 'fille dangereuse et artificielle', accused her of duplicity, and declared that she had opened his eyes to the character of women. Though writing in the privacy of his Journal, he was bitterly on the defensive. His statement that her candour and her expressions of tenderness gave him feelings of 'regret and almost of remorse' seems to be ironical, but it is obvious that he had been deeply moved. He did not allow his remorse to interfere with his studies, however, and in his Journal he reports his day's reading as usual.

Gibbon sincerely wished to forget Suzanne, but he found to his sorrow that she was not easily forgotten. In February 1764 she arrived in Lausanne for a stay of six weeks. Gibbon was then amusing himself by flirting conspicuously with a young Swiss woman named Madame Seigneux, but in his Journal he mentions Suzanne a score of times. He confesses that he could not help thinking about her a great deal, and that he saw her three or four times a week. Though he insists that he made it clear to her a hundred times that the past was irrevocable, he makes it clear to us that he simply could not keep away from her. He was ill at ease in her presence, however, and it infuriated him that she should be calmer and more her old self than he. He wrote highly uncomplimentary remarks about her in his Journal, protesting too often and too vigorously that he was completely cured of his love for her.* At

---

Jean-Jacques; but that extraordinary man, whom I admire and pity, should have been less precipitate in condemning the moral character and conduct of a stranger.' (Murray, *Autobiographies*, 298.)

* Not long after Suzanne's arrival in Lausanne Gibbon accompanied her to a performance of *Zaïre* in Voltaire's theatre at Mon Repos — a suburb of Lausanne. In his Journal he remarked that 'at the most interesting passages of *Zaïre* she sobbed so loudly that all eyes turned to her. Yet when she took away

last, however, Suzanne returned to Geneva, and a few days later Gibbon departed for Italy.

Then came the final act in Suzanne's great romance. In June 1764 she became the paid companion of a young widow who took her to Paris. Here her employer had been receiving the attentions of a rich banker from Geneva, Jacques Necker, but the banker now transferred his affections to the companion, and before the end of the year he had married Suzanne. She made him an excellent wife. Her *salon* was one of the most brilliant in Paris; she helped her husband to rise to the position of finance minister to Louis XVI (1776–8 and 1788–90); and in the early days of the French Revolution he was one of the most popular men in France. Moreover, as soon as Suzanne was safely married to a millionaire, Gibbon no longer considered her dangerous and full of artifice. On his way home from Italy (June 1765) he stopped in Paris for ten days. Suzanne invited him to supper every evening and she was delighted to let him see her new position in the world.

In later years the former lovers became warm friends. They saw much of each other when the Neckers visited London in 1776, and when Gibbon visited Paris a year later Suzanne arranged a triumphal welcome for him. On his departure from this visit he wrote her that her friendship 'fait le consolation et la gloire de ma vie'. In the autumn of 1783, when Gibbon established his residence in Lausanne, the Neckers were living at Rolle, where he visited them, and they passed the summer of 1784 at Lausanne. After Necker's fall from power in France (1790) he and Suzanne made their home at Coppet, near Geneva, and later at Rolle, where they

---

her handkerchief we saw only a fresh and happy face, with no signs of tears. Everyone noticed so crude an affectation. How this girl plays with sensibility.' In Voltaire's play, Zaïre, betrothed to the sultan Orosmane, is unjustly accused of infidelity because of his misunderstanding of a letter intercepted by one of his slaves. He murders her, becomes convinced of her innocence, and commits suicide. Gibbon commented in his Journal upon the 'frightful cruelty of Orosmane', but apparently it did not occur to him or to Suzanne to say, *Mutato nomine de te fabula narratur*. Or perhaps Suzanne did see the parallel, and aimed her sobs at Gibbon.

saw Gibbon frequently. In one of her letters to Gibbon Suzanne called herself his 'première et dernière amie', adding that she could not decide which of these titles she found 'le plus doux et le plus chère à mon coeur'. Five months after receiving this letter Gibbon died, and Suzanne's death followed a few weeks later. Shortly before the end she learned from Lord Sheffield that Gibbon had mentioned her in his Memoirs, and she died assured that she had indeed been his first and last *amie*.

Until almost the end of the nineteenth century students of Gibbon's life had only Lord Sheffield's edition of the Memoirs and a few letters to guide them. As Gibbon devoted barely two pages to his love affair with Suzanne Curchod, his early biographers and critics dismissed the episode as trivial and of little consequence, and as the Memoirs do not mention her at all in their account of Gibbon's second stay in Lausanne (was this silence due to his being ashamed of his conduct?), it was generally assumed that the affair ended when Gibbon sighed as a lover and obeyed as a son. In fact the best of these early biographers suggests that if Gibbon mentioned the affair at all, it was only because Suzanne was the prominent Madame Necker at the time he wrote his Memoirs.[9] The gradual publication of Gibbon's letters and Journal, between 1880 and 1956, showed how wrong these biographers had been. It is now perfectly clear that Gibbon and Suzanne loved each other deeply, and that neither of them ever forgot this early love. Moreover the most important part of the story came after their engagement had been broken, for this love affair had permanent effects upon the historian's character — effects which may be seen even in the History itself.

That Gibbon was essentially a kind-hearted person is abundantly proved by his dealings with his father, his stepmother, Sheffield and his wife and daughter, the Séverys (in Lausanne in the 1780s), Deyverdun, and Suzanne herself. He might be annoyed at times, but his anger soon passed. There can be no doubt that he was distressed by Suzanne's pleading letters and that he was very angry with his stepmother for intercepting one of them. He wrote to Suzanne that he could hardly refrain from overwhelming his stepmother with reproaches when he learned that she had made him wait six months for the reply to his most important letter. He held no lasting grudge against his stepmother, however, and at this time he blamed no one for the collapse of his dreams. But more than four years later he suddenly began accusing Suzanne of duplicity. Why? We know that he first made this charge when he unexpectedly encountered her at Ferney in August 1763, and that it was her hysterical defence of her conduct, received six weeks later, that inspired him to write the following disjointed comment in his Journal:

> [September 22]. I have received a most unexpected letter. It was from Mademoiselle C. A dangerous girl, full of artifice! Because of the air of candour which pervades your letter, and the sentiments of tenderness and honesty which you display, I felt regret and almost remorse. She made a defence of her conduct from the first moment that she knew me, affirming her constancy to me, her scorn for M. de Montplaisir, and the tender and firm fidelity which she believed she observed in the letter in which I notified her there was no longer any hope. Her journeys to Lausanne, the admirers whom she had there, and the complaisance with which she listened to them, are very difficult to justify. Neither d'Eyverdun (she says) nor anybody else has for a moment effaced my image from her heart. She amused herself at Lausanne, but without being attached to anyone there. Granted. Nevertheless, these amusements still convict her of the most odious dissimulation, and if infidelity is sometimes a weakness, duplicity is always a vice. In the month of July 1758 she wrote me a strange letter from Crassy, full of tenderness and despair, reporting that her eyes were filled with tears, her health enfeebled by grief. In that same month of July she was at Lausanne, full of health and charm, *the object of the women's jealousy and the sighs of the men*, enjoying every form of pleasure, founding Academies, distributing prizes, bandying

> witticisms, and playing with love, even if she did not engage herself seriously. Is not this contrast enough to enlighten me as to her character? I say enlighten. It is only a question of ideas and not at all of feelings. The most complete justification, while restoring my esteem for her, could no longer rekindle fires that are completely extinguished. As she tells me that she must soon leave Geneva, I shall not see her again, and all is finished.[10]

How are we to explain this very unjust attack upon Suzanne? Gibbon had made no such charges at any time before his second stay at Lausanne, and we must wonder why he made them then. We can only guess at an explanation. Gibbon knew that he could never marry Suzanne and, after a painful struggle lasting several months, he had succeeded in forgetting her — more or less. Such self-discipline was relatively easy in England, where there was nothing to remind him of her, but at Lausanne everything awakened old memories. He therefore became alarmed, and as he was determined not to go through the old struggle again, he feared Suzanne and, more especially, he feared himself. Acting in self-defence, he told her brutally and frequently that all was over between them, and to make sure of himself he tried desperately to convince himself that she was unworthy of him. He attributed to her the unpleasant qualities of the wicked woman in a romantic tragedy.

But upon what evidence did Gibbon charge Suzanne with such duplicity? Friends in Lausanne had written him of her gay social life there in July 1758, but she protested her innocence, and we know of nothing in her conduct to justify a charge of infidelity. Moreover Gibbon did not lay great emphasis upon this aspect of her conduct. His charge was that she had written him a heart-rending letter, luridly describing her sufferings, but that at that very time she was enjoying herself to the full at Lausanne. She must therefore have lied to him about her lacerated feelings. Obviously he was referring to her letter of 7 September, actually written at Crassy more than a month after her return from Lausanne, and only a day or two after she received his letter of 24 August, in which he broke their engagement. But how did Gibbon come to believe that this letter was written in July? The editor of his letters points out that at the end of her letter Suzanne wrote the date 'ce 7me 7bre', and plausibly suggests that Gibbon misread the 7bre (septembre) as meaning July — the seventh month.[11] This misreading was made the easier by his stepmother, who intercepted the letter and did not show it to him until several months later. At the time it did not occur to him to associate Suzanne's letter with her activities of the preceding July, but more than four years later, when fear was driving him to seek complaints against her, he remembered the letter, whose confusing date line persuaded him that the gay life at Lausanne had followed immediately upon the breaking of their engagement. When Suzanne's marriage to M. Necker relieved him of his fear of her, he no longer charged her with duplicity. But more than a quarter of a century later, when he was on the friendliest terms with her, he solemnly recorded in his Memoirs[12] that 'my cure was accelerated by a faithful report of the tranquillity and chearfulness of the Lady herself'. He had long since forgotten his own story of a trip to Fribourg and Berne, but he could not forget or cease to believe his false charge that Suzanne had lied to him.

At the close of his denunciation of Suzanne's alleged duplicity Gibbon permitted himself a line or two of moralizing in his Journal. 'This affair,' he wrote,[13] 'so remarkable in all its aspects, has been very useful to me. It has opened my eyes to the character of women, and it will serve me for a long time as a protection against the seductions of love.' Only rarely does Gibbon descend to such shopworn banalities as these, and his lapse on this occasion is instructive: he had been deeply hurt, angered, and frightened by Suzanne's letters, but he really believed what he was writing in his Journal, and he took no pains to say it elegantly. As he had been living in the world for twenty-six years, and had served in the army for two years and a half, he presumably had, on occasion, heard men express cynical views regarding women. But his charges against Suzanne were no barrack-room jests: they came from a full heart. When Gibbon outgrew his bitterness towards Suzanne, he continued to charge women in general with duplicity, though reproach often was mellowed into ridicule and witticisms about cuckolds. With him 'love' became a dirty word. His many jests on the subject, we may be sure, are evidence of a secret fear inspired by his personal experience with alleged feminine deceit.

A few months after his return to England, Gibbon wrote to Holroyd, crowing about his successes with the Neckers at Paris. 'Could they insult me more cruelly?' he asked facetiously. 'Ask me every evening to supper, go to bed and leave me alone with his wife; what an impertinent security. It is making an old lover of mighty little consequence.' A year later, in a letter to a Swiss friend, Gibbon permitted himself to develop with wit and at considerable length the thesis that, in love affairs, it is better to make other men dupes than to be one yourself, and that a sensible but honest man of refinement will prefer married women to young girls who might fall in love with him. It was only a few years later that Gibbon wrote the first of many passages in *The Decline and Fall* that deal with cuckolds.[14] He is speaking of Faustina, wife of the Emperor Marcus Aurelius. 'Marcus was the only man in the empire who seemed ignorant or insensible of the irregularities of Faustina; which, according to the prejudices of every age, reflected some disgrace on the injured husband.' To this remark Gibbon appended a footnote: 'The world has laughed at the credulity of Marcus; but Madame Dacier assures us (and we may credit a lady) that the husband will always be deceived, if the wife condescends to dissemble.' Marcus is only the first of a long procession of injured husbands who file through Gibbon's pages, and at each of them the author snickers and seems to say, 'There, but for the timely warning I received, go I, Edward Gibbon!'

We must also ask how much protection Gibbon needed 'against the seductions of love'. Probably not very much, for he had virtually no sex life, either before or after his purely platonic romance with

Suzanne. Raised by a maiden aunt, debilitated by childhood illnesses, lonely and out of touch with his fellow students at Oxford, and completing his adolescence in the home of a Calvinist clergyman in puritan Lausanne, he was not compassed about by lurid temptations in his youth, and at that time his deportment was exemplary. But except in the case of Suzanne he never thought of marrying. In fact he showed fright at the very thought of marriage. On more than one occasion during the next quarter of a century his stepmother or Lady Sheffield thought she had found him a suitable wife, but we hear nothing of a serious attachment on his part. While he still was in the militia his stepmother paraded a few young ladies before him, but to no avail. Regarding one of them he wrote in his Journal: 'She is a pretty, meek (but I am afraid) insipid Girl. She has been talked of for me, but tho' she will have a noble fortune, I must have a wife I can speak to.'[15] In this matter Suzanne had set standards which very few English girls could meet. In his last years at Lausanne he greatly enjoyed the society of women, young or old, and even became something of a flirt, but he valued these women chiefly as appreciative listeners to his conversation.

When he was in the army, however, and during his early days in London, he lived in a very different atmosphere; he was lonely, and he was subjected to new temptations. As he remarked in his Memoirs many years later:

> The pleasures of a town life, the daily round from the tavern to the play, from the play to the coffee-house, from the coffee-house to the Bagnio are within the reach of every man who is regardless of his health, his money, and his company. By the contagion of example I was sometimes seduced; but the better habits which I had formed at Lausanne induced me to seek a more rational and elegant society . . .[16]

The vague and somewhat boastful form of this confession makes us wonder how far he descended along the primrose path. Probably not very far. Once, and only once, does he hint at such a descent in his Journal. There can be little doubt that the army had coarsened his manners and morals, particularly by leading him to drink too much, but hostile critics go too far when they attack him because of alleged relations with women.

In his account of his Parisian friend, Madame Bontems, written more than twenty-five years after the events in question and deleted by Lord Sheffield from his edition of the Memoirs, Gibbon slyly insinuates that he shared her favours with the Marquis de Mirabeau, who 'was neither her first nor her last lover'. Gibbon's detractors have made much of this 'guilty love', but if they were to read the account of her in his Journal, written only a few weeks after he left Paris, they would be sorely disillusioned. 'She talked to me of sensual pleasures,' he records,[17] 'encouraged me to speak of them, and listened to me read the fables of La Fontaine; and when, excited by these teasings, I took a few liberties, she repulsed me feebly and seemed excited. Avec un peu plus de hardiesse j'aurois peut être reussi.' These last words would seem to settle the matter, and it is clear that they should be translated, 'Had I been a little bolder, *she* might perhaps have succeeded.' Madame Bontems was the unsuccessful aggressor.

A few months later, at Lausanne, Gibbon made the acquaintance of a young Swiss woman named Madame Seigneux. She was bored by her husband, and for about six weeks she and Gibbon carried on a brisk flirtation. On one occasion Gibbon confided darkly to his Journal, after describing a visit to her, 'I have no designs, but if I had, I am sure that only the opportunity would be lacking.' A few days later he described the climax of their intrigue as follows: 'You should have seen her standing near the stove, her lustful eyes half closed, allowing me to slip my arms around her and to put my mouth on hers.' A man of twenty-six who, in the secrecy of his Journal, makes so much of having put his arms around a woman and kissed her can scarcely have been a widely experienced Casanova. Nevertheless Gibbon's flirtation with 'la petite femme' attracted such attention that Suzanne took it upon herself to warn him that his conduct was ruining his reputation. Three days later he wrote, 'Je me refroidis.' While at Milan he wrote a long letter to Holroyd, who was still at Lausanne, at the close of which he asked for 'some account of the said little woman, whether she talks bawdy as much as usual, and who is my successor'. That was all.[18]

Further light is thrown on this aspect of Gibbon's character by the obscenity — *une obscénité érudite et froide*, according to the French critic Sainte-Beuve — of many passages in the History. In a careful and justly famous criticism of *The Decline and Fall*, Gibbon's contemporary, the Cambridge classical scholar Richard Porson, complained of 'that rage for indecency which pervades the whole work, but especially the last volumes'. He then went on to declare that 'If the History were anonymous, I should guess that these disgraceful obscenities were written by some debauchee, who having from age, or accident, or excess, survived the practice of lust, still indulged himself in the luxury of speculation; and exposed the impotent imbecility, after he had lost the vigour, of the passions.'[19]

Perhaps the learned professor guessed better than he knew. Gibbon certainly was no worn-out debauchee, but we can state with equal assurance that he was definitely undersexed, perhaps in consequence of his childhood illnesses. Such impotence would help us explain his lifelong aversion to marriage, his boastings in old age about real or imaginary escapades in his youth (at London and with Madame Bontems), his witticisms about oversexed women (notably the Empresses Faustina and Theodora), and the 'cold and erudite obscenity' that pervades his writings.

CHAPTER FOUR

'FROM SUPERSTITION TO SCEPTICISM'

AMONG the books in Gibbon's library was a large and well-thumbed Bible whose title-page bore the date 1663. On the back of this page was written, in a large childish hand, the one word: 'Edward'.[1] How this book came into the historian's possession we do not know, but the date and signature suggest that it had once belonged to his grandfather, the first Edward Gibbon. This grandfather belonged to a religious family. His brother, Thomas Gibbon (1668/9–1715), entered Holy orders and eventually became Dean of Carlisle; his daughter Hester Gibbon (1705–90) passed the greater part of her life as a religious recluse; and how deeply his grandson, the historian, shared the family preoccupation with religion and theology is shown in his writings. Further evidence of the grandfather's interest in religion may be seen in his patronage of the illustrious William Law.

William Law (1686–1761) was one of the most remarkable men to appear in the English Church during the eighteenth century. He was famous as a scholar, a wit, and a controversialist, and he was often considered a saint. When he became a fellow of Emmanuel College, Cambridge, in 1711, it seemed that a brilliant career in the Church lay open before him, but three years later he sacrificed all hope of preferment by refusing to swear allegiance to England's new king, George I, the founder of the Hanoverian dynasty. Throughout life Law remained a Jacobite, a non-juror, a critic of Deism, and a defender of High Church doctrine; in his later years he was impressed by the writings of the German mystic, Jakob Böhme (1575–1624); and he is remembered today primarily for his devotional and mystical writings.

Attracted to Law, no doubt by his Jacobitism and his High Church piety, the elder Gibbon employed the non-juror as his personal chaplain, the spiritual director of his family, and the tutor of his son (1723). For seventeen years Law lived with the Gibbons at Putney, but he was always more than a rich man's private chaplain. He was a national figure as a counsellor of youth, visited by a steady procession of serious young men seeking inspiration. Among these visitors were John and Charles Wesley and several others who were later to be numbered among the founders of Methodism. It was while living with the Gibbons at Putney that Law wrote his most important books, including the *Serious Call to a Devout and Holy Life* (1728). This famous work exercised an abiding influence upon the religious life of England, remaining a popular favourite for more than a hundred years, but for us its special interest lies in its character sketches of various types of religious and irreligious persons. In three of these sketches the historian hesitatingly claimed to recognize his father and his two aunts: 'Flatus' (supposedly the historian's father) is pictured as a drifter who never amounts to much because he lacks strong principles, while 'Flavia' (Gibbon's aunt, Katharine Elliston, whose daughter became Lady Eliot) and 'Miranda' (his other aunt, Hester Gibbon) are depicted as the pagan and the true Christian respectively.[2]

About three years after his patron's death in 1736, Law withdrew from the Gibbon household and returned to his native village in Northamptonshire. Perhaps he had quarrelled with his pupil, now head of the Gibbon family, but perhaps he merely wished to practise the mystical life more freely than was possible at Putney. Hester Gibbon soon followed him to his retreat, where she spent the remainder of her life caring for him and performing works of charity and devotion. In 1761 Law died in the house ('I may not say in the arms', her nephew candidly confessed) of his admiring Miranda, but not until 1790 did death enable her to be buried at her hero's side.

The historian was only three years old when Law left Putney;

probably he never again set eyes upon the great non-juror; and he saw his Aunt Hester only rarely and briefly. There can therefore be no question of a direct influence of Law upon Gibbon, though the historian reports in his Memoirs that as a child he had been taught to regard Law as 'a worthy and pious man, who believed all that he professed and practised all that he enjoyned'. Presumably the principal agent in transmitting this favourable image of Law was Catherine Porten, the 'Aunt Kitty' from whom Gibbon received most of his early education. We know very little about Miss Porten's religion, but though she certainly was not the woman to follow Hester Gibbon into the wilderness, she can hardly have escaped completely from Law's influence during the years when they both lived at Purney.

Gibbon declared that from childhood he and his aunt had engaged in religious disputation, and he reports that she was often 'puzzled by my objections to the mysteries she strove to believe'. He does not inform us which mysteries these were, but we may safely assume that she taught her nephew the customary High Anglican doctrines and practices, with a strong dash of Law thrown in. At any rate, when Gibbon arrived at Oxford at the age of fifteen his childhood faith was still intact; he signed the Thirty-nine Articles without a qualm (though he later denied it, perhaps by a slip of memory, or perhaps in order to make a point against Oxford[3]); he believed in miracles; he revered the saints and fathers of the Church; and he 'groped his way' to the communion table in the Magdalen College chapel. Like other members of his family, Gibbon had a religious nature, and he was as yet untouched by doubt.

During his tedious second year at Oxford Gibbon stumbled upon Conyers Middleton's recent *Free Enquiry* (1749). After scrutinizing the evidence for the miraculous powers allegedly enjoyed by the Christian Church during the first four or five centuries of its history the author of this book concluded that the Church had never possessed such powers. Middleton's radical scepticism, expressed in strong and persuasive language, aroused alarm in ecclesiastical circles; numerous replies and confutations of his book were published; and Gibbon charges that Oxford conferred honorary degrees upon the 'two dullest' of his critics. The notoriety of this infidel book induced Gibbon to procure and read it, and this reading altered the whole subsequent course of his life.

The immediate effect of Middleton's book upon young Gibbon was exactly the opposite of that which its author would have desired. Instead of renouncing belief in the miracles supposedly wrought in apostolic and post-apostolic times, Gibbon decided that, if he accepted the miracles of the early Church, he must also accept many ancient dogmas and practices that all Protestants — even High Church Anglicans — had long since discarded as Romish distortions of the true Gospel. Middleton showed that these alleged innovations were as well authenticated as the biblical miracles which Gibbon was unwilling to reject. He therefore began crossing himself, adored images and relics, and invoked the saints, soon surpassing even his Aunt Hester in such practices; he admitted the superior merits of celibacy and the monastic life; and before long he accepted the Catholic doctrines of purgatory and transubstantiation.

Gibbon then happened to make the acquaintance of a fellow student at Magdalen whose views on religion resembled his own. This companion lent him a few Catholic books, and within three months Gibbon had read himself into the Roman Church. In his Memoirs[4] he reports that the books were Bossuet's *Exposition of the Catholic Doctrine* and his *History of the Variations of the Protestant Churches*, but he told Lord Sheffield that he was persuaded by the writings of Robert Parsons (or Persons), an English Jesuit who had lived in the days of Queen Elizabeth. Possibly he read both authors, and others as well. We can be sure, however, that he had only a reader's knowledge of the Roman Church and its tenets. He had never known a Catholic or talked with one about religion;[5] he may never have seen a Catholic church; and he almost certainly had never attended a Catholic mass. If he ever did attend mass it must have been in the day or two between his admission to the Church and the arrival of his irate father, who dragged him off to Putney, preparatory to banishing him to Lausanne.

When he came to write his Memoirs, Gibbon pictured his conversion as a purely rational affair, laying the blame on Bossuet's powerful reasoning, and proudly declaring, 'I surely fell by a noble hand.' Parsons's arguments usually were on a more emotional level, appealing to the courage and enthusiasm of youth, and eloquently urging the necessity of immediate action. Such exhortations may have hurried Gibbon to his hasty decision. Mention must also be made, in passing, of another factor that may have somewhat facilitated his conversion. Gibbon always showed a strong feeling for family, and he doubtless knew that three of his Acton cousins[6] had been converted to Catholicism; two of these cousins had been Catholics for many years, but Sir Whitmore Acton had only recently been converted. Conversion to Catholicism was not an unheard-of event in Gibbon's family. But the fundamental factors in Gibbon's conversion were his religious nature and his romantic imagination, stimulated by his loneliness at Magdalen.

As soon as he had convinced himself that Catholic doctrine was true, Gibbon made haste to profess himself a Catholic. He managed to find a Jesuit priest attached to the Sardinian embassy in London, and at this man's feet he solemnly 'abjured the errors of heresy' (8 June 1753). The young convert then composed a letter to his father, announcing what had happened. The letter has been lost, but many years later its author assured his friend Holroyd that it was 'written with all the pomp, the dignity, and self-satisfaction of a martyr'[7] — which seems to reflect the influence of Parsons rather than that of Bossuet.

A few days later Gibbon was hustled off to Lausanne for reconversion to Protestantism. As he knew only a little French, and his Swiss tutor, M. Pavillard, was even less familiar with English, they found it impossible at first to carry on serious theological discussions, but as soon as Gibbon had an adequate command of

French, Pavillard began engaging his pupil in long debates, pointing out to him the various weaknesses in the Catholic position. Several years later Pavillard described to Holroyd[8] 'the astonishment with which he gazed on Mr. Gibbon standing before him: a thin little figure, with a large head, disputing and urging, with the greatest ability, all the best arguments that had ever been used in favour of popery'. Pavillard gradually won the great debate, but Gibbon always insisted, correctly no doubt, that really he reconverted himself. In his Memoirs he tells us how he came to reject the doctrine of transubstantiation,* after which 'the various articles of the Romish creed disappeared like a dream'; but Pavillard, writing to Gibbon's father at the time, reported that each major Catholic doctrine had to be argued separately and at length, before his pupil would surrender it.[9] Pavillard's version is indubitably the correct one.

At last Gibbon was ready to take the decisive step. After formally requesting that he be admitted to communion in the Protestant Church, and after being examined as to his faith and morals by a committee of its clergy, he received the sacrament from the hands of M. Pavillard in the Protestant cathedral at Lausanne. The ceremony took place on Christmas Day 1754, slightly over a year and a half after his conversion to Catholicism. A few days later, in January 1755, Pavillard notified Gibbon's father of the boy's

* '... it [Gibbon's reconversion] was principally effected by my private reflexions, and I still remember my solitary transport at the discovery of a philosophical argument against the doctrine of transubstantian [*sic*]: *that* the text of scripture, which seems to inculcate the real presence, is attested only by a single sense — our sight; while the real presence itself is disproved by three of our senses — the sight, the touch, and the taste.' (Murray, 137). This passage is of interest as showing how shallow was Gibbon's knowledge of Catholic theology, both in 1754 and in 1789 when he wrote these words. He even introduced this argument into *The Decline and Fall* (VI, 131), though any informed Catholic could have told him that sight, touch, and taste cannot perceive the 'substance' of the bread and wine, and that, according to Catholic theology, this 'substance' is all that changes during the celebration of the mass. Gibbon did not understand this cardinal doctrine of Catholicism. He had read books on Catholic theology and Catholic arguments against Protestantism, but as he never had an opportunity to discuss them with a Catholic, he understood them in his own way, which was not always the Catholic way.

reconversion, and at the same time Gibbon wrote to his Aunt Kitty: 'I am now good protestant & am extremely glad of it.'[10] These last five words certainly were true and they were the most significant part of his letter. At long last Gibbon had thrown off the incubus that had caused him to be exiled from his college, his family, and his country, and which he had long been forcing himself to defend against Pavillard's sustained and skilful attacks. No wonder he felt relieved when the struggles were over.

In later years Gibbon was rather ashamed of his brief flirtation with Catholicism and rarely talked about it, even to close friends. Lord Sheffield assures us that during the thirty years of their intimate friendship he heard Gibbon speak of it only once. But thirty-five years after the event, when he came to write his Memoirs, he could not pass silently over the immediate cause of his momentous exile to Lausanne. He therefore declared that 'I now smile or blush at the recollection of my folly'; wrote an account of it in language that was unnecessarily anti-Catholic; paid himself a few high compliments ('Youth is sincere and impetuous, and a momentary glow of Enthusiasm had raised me above all temporal considerations', and 'I am proud of an honest sacrifice of interest to conscience'); laid the blame on Oxford; quoted a few lines from Dryden (a distinguished convert to Catholicism); and devoted several pages to comparing himself to Chillingworth (1602–44) and Bayle (1647–1706). (Each of these famous men had been 'seduced by similar sophistry to embrace the same system of superstition', but each quickly returned to Protestantism, and each eventually fell into deep scepticism.) After thus defending his conversion and reconversion, Gibbon closed the discussion by remarking that 'It was here that I suspended my Religious enquiries, acquiescing with implicit belief in the tenets and mysteries which are adopted by the general consent of Catholics and Protestants'.[11]

In spite of this statement (first made in 1790) we can be sure that Gibbon did not suspend his religious inquiries on Christmas Day

1754. For several years thereafter he remained a good Protestant, at least in outward appearance. He was still the pupil of a Calvinist clergyman, for whom he always expressed the highest esteem, and when he left Lausanne in 1758 he looked forward to marrying Suzanne Curchod, the pious daughter of another Calvinist clergyman. Many difficulties beset these young lovers, but differences regarding religion were not among them. After his return to England Gibbon quietly followed the religious routine of a conventional country squire, ordinarily accompanying his parents to the Buriton parish church twice every Sunday. But both Journal and Memoirs tell us[12] that he used the occasion principally to improve his Greek by following the Lessons in a Greek Bible which he kept in the family pew. In his Memoirs, Gibbon adds that during the sermon he ordinarily meditated on the Scripture that had just been read, and he reports that his mind was often disturbed by difficulties and doubts which the biblical commentaries in Law's library could not resolve. The Journal knows nothing of such doubts, but it contains several favourable comments on the sermons he heard. Gibbon listened to them more attentively than the Memoirs suggest, and he still was a good Protestant.

Even during his years at Lausanne, however, Gibbon began his slow but sure advance along the road to scepticism, and, strange as it may seem, the first manifestations of this critical spirit were caused by the zeal of M. Pavillard. In September 1755 the Pavillards and Gibbon toured Switzerland, with the pastor always making sure that his pupil had ample opportunity to observe the superstition then prevalent in the Catholic cantons. When reporting upon the trip to Gibbon's father, Pavillard declared himself extremely gratified by the vigour with which the boy expressed disgust at what he saw.[13]

Young Gibbon was especially impressed and disgusted by the famous monastery at Einsiedeln, near Zürich. This monastery was located in a poverty-stricken corner of Europe, but its monks paraded their enormous wealth with an ostentation that Gibbon never forgot. In an account of the trip written soon after his return to Lausanne, he dwelt at length upon their vain display of wealth; he ridiculed the various miracles they reported; and he pronounced their monastery to be 'at once a triumph of superstition, a masterpiece of ecclesiastical scheming, and a disgrace to mankind'.[14] Nine years later he levelled similar charges against the cathedral at Milan, commenting that its riches 'only prove the trickery of the Church and the folly of our forebears'. He denounced the wealth of Einsiedeln again in his unpublished *History of the Swiss Republic* (1767), speaking contemptuously of 'these monks who were religious only in name' and of the 'superstition which still attracts crowds of pilgrims and offerings'. In his unfinished *Antiquities of the House of Brunswick* (1790) he has his fun with the miracles at Einsiedeln, which he here calls 'the Loretto of Switzerland'. He does not mention Einsiedeln in *The Decline and Fall*, though he returns time and time again to the avarice and venality of priests and monks. And finally, he once more describes his youthful visit to Einsiedeln in his Memoirs, commenting upon its 'lively naked image of superstition', which he 'viewed with the contempt of a protestant and a philosopher'.[15]

During the remaining years of his stay in Lausanne Gibbon wrote a number of essays on religious topics, often accusing the clergy of greed and ambition, and denying the truth of alleged prophecies and miracles. In an essay written early in 1756, for example, he noted a number of resemblances between the druids, as described by Caesar, and the Catholic clergy of his own day, from which he concluded that the clergy of all times and all peoples are essentially alike. Towards the end of the same year he was studying the chronological difficulties presented by the prophecies of Daniel, and in an essay written in 1757 he criticized two prophecies reported by Suetonius, declaring that a philosopher must regard all such stories as 'sorry evidence of the political craft of the powerful, the gullibility of the populace, the adulation of historians, and the fraud of priests'. Serious study, he added, would lead to 'in-

The Parish Church at Fletching, Sussex, three miles from Sheffield Place. Gibbon's remains lie in Lord Sheffield's vault in the north transept

credulity but a wise and enlightened incredulity, of which more than one saint and more than one father of the church has stood in need'.[16]

The direction of Gibbon's thinking on theological matters at this time is further illustrated in a letter he addressed to a professor at Zürich in January 1757. After filling six large pages with discussions of various Latin texts, Gibbon concluded his letter by writing:

> Now I should like to ask a favour of you, Most Learned Sir. A friend of mine has prepared some criticisms of a book recently published under the title, '*Lettres sur le Déisme par M. le Pr. Salchi de Lausanne*'. His criticisms are written with a certain liberty, though not irresponsibly, and he would like to have them published in your distinguished journal, the Museum Helveticum. I earnestly beg you to accede to his wish, for such liberties are necessary if the cause of literature is to prosper.

In due time the professor replied that he would have been glad to publish the essay had not the Journal suspended publication three years before. As Salchi, a professor of Hebrew in Lausanne, had attacked the English Deists in his *Letters*, Gibbon's friend presumably sympathized with Deism, and we may strongly suspect that this 'friend' was none other than Gibbon himself.[17]

At this time Gibbon read widely in books of an unorthodox character, apparently taking great delight in their authors' attacks upon the Church and its priesthood. Many years later, when writing his Memoirs, he recollected that Giannone's *Civil History of Naples* had reinforced his low opinion of the Catholic clergy; that the Abbé de la Bléterie's *Life of Julian* had inspired him to write an essay, now lost, in which he cast doubt upon the miracle that supposedly dissuaded Julian from rebuilding the Jewish temple at Jerusalem; and that he 'learned to manage the weapon of grave and temperate irony, even on subjects of Ecclesiastical solemnity', by a frequent reading and re-reading of Pascal's *Provincial Letters*.

There can be little doubt that his pleasure in reading such books arose from the fact that they set forth his own ideas better than he could then express them himself.[18]

Critics often make the very doubtful assumption that, in accusing the Catholic Church and its clergy of avarice and superstition, Gibbon was merely echoing the fashion of the day, as set by Voltaire and the French encyclopedists. It is true that Voltaire was living near Lausanne in 1757 and 1758, and that Gibbon, being a young Englishman of fortune, easily procured an invitation to meet the great man. At the time Gibbon was proud of his achievement and sometimes spoke grandiloquently of 'my friend Voltaire', but he admired his 'friend' as a poet and dramatist, not as a historian or a critic of religion, and presently he changed his mind. After reading *The Age of Louis XIV* in 1762, he attacked its author severely in his Journal, and in the notes to *The Decline and Fall* he pounces with joy upon Voltaire's numerous mistakes in history and geography, speaking ironically of his 'pious zeal' (which he pronounced 'excessive and even ridiculous'), and finally dismissing him with 'In his way Voltaire was a bigot, an intolerant bigot.'[19] Gibbon may have taken a few minor ideas and a few well-turned phrases from Voltaire, but that is all. The encyclopedists exercised even less influence upon Gibbon, who, even before he left Lausanne, had begun writing an essay in which he criticized various ideas set forth by d'Alembert in his famous 'Discours préliminaire' to the *Encyclopédie*.

The winters of 1758 and 1759, which Gibbon passed in London, witnessed a further development of his ideas concerning religion. He frequently saw his father's old friend David Mallet, in whose house he had stayed before his departure for Lausanne. Mallet was an aggressive Deist whose remarks had scandalized rather than reclaimed the young convert, but five years later Gibbon was better prepared to receive strong doctrine. In addition to listening sympathetically to Mallet, he again took up Conyers Middleton, the writer whose scepticism had once scared him into the Catholic

Church, and it apparently was at this time that he first came upon Hume's *Natural History of Religion* and his 'Essay on Miracles'. While in the militia Gibbon went through six volumes by the French sceptic Fontenelle, whose influence upon him was greater than Voltaire's and, he dipped into the *Dictionnaire historique et critique* by Pierre Bayle, the first of the eighteenth-century sceptics. And finally, Gibbon tells us in his Memoirs that in 1759 his reading of Grotius's *De Veritate Religiònis Christianae*[20] led him to make 'a regular tryal of the evidence of Christianity'. This 'tryal' left him a convinced sceptic in matters of religion.

The advance of Gibbon's theological scepticism may be traced a step further in his *Essai sur l'étude de la littérature*. This little book's earlier chapters show no concern with religion, but the last third of the book, written in 1761, is given over entirely to an examination of ancient paganism. Here Gibbon sets forth many fundamental ideas to which he adhered thereafter. After rejecting the widely held theory that the pagan deities were ancient heroes who had earned divinity by their services to humanity, Gibbon maintained (perhaps developing upon suggestions drawn from Hume) that these gods were personifications of the forces of nature, of which primitive men always stood in awe.

During the next few years Gibbon repeatedly mentioned religion in his Journal. Thus in 1763 he wrote: 'For the man who can raise himself above the prejudices of party and sect, the history of Religions is the most interesting part of the History of the human Spirit.' A few months later, while at Florence, he read a translation of the 'Edda', which he called 'the sacred book of the ancient Celts'. He then commented: 'We now have a half dozen bibles (including our own). A valuable work might be written, giving a Philosophic picture of these Religions, their Spirit, their reasonings, and their influence on the manners, government, Philosophy and Poetry of each people.'[21] In these passages, and similar ones, Gibbon made it clear that he had come to regard the religions of the world, including Christianity, as interesting social phenomena to be explained by a study of their origins and history. He was a historian and a scholar, not a believer.

Throughout his life Gibbon continued to denounce 'superstition' and 'fanaticism', and to insist that these evils can be conquered only by reason and toleration. 'Fanaticism', he wrote in his Journal, 'is one of those epidemic diseases of the human Spirit which merit great attention', and on another page, 'Intolerant superstition is even more dangerous than impiety.' When Richard Hurd (tutor to George IV and later an Anglican bishop) published (1772) a book defending prophecy, Gibbon wrote him a long but anonymous letter warning him that 'if we cast aside this buckler [scepticism], the blind fury of superstition, from every age of the world, and from every corner of the globe, will invade us naked and unarmed'. When Protestant mobs attacked Catholics during the Gordon riots of 1780 he spoke angrily of 'the old story of religion'.[22]

When Gibbon read Voltaire's *Traité sur la tolérance*, soon after its publication in 1763, he commented, 'Its purpose is entirely laudable: to awaken in every heart the sentiment of humanity and to show the frightful consequences of superstition', but he went on to say that the book was merely 'a collection of commonplaces'.[23] Gibbon never took up Voltaire's battle cry against the Church — 'Écrasez l'infâme!' — for he considered it a form of bigotry, and bigotry against religion was, in his opinion, just as bad as bigotry in its favour. He even went so far as to state, in his Memoirs, that during his first visit to Paris, in 1763, he was disgusted by the 'intolerant zeal' of Holbach and his friends, who laughed at the mild scepticism of Hume and 'rashly pronounced that every man must be either an Atheist or a fool'.[24] In his Journal, however, he recorded no such remarks and showed no signs of such disgust.

Gibbon was an urbane, tolerant, and enlightened sceptic, thoroughly at home in the polished and sceptical society of the eighteenth century. Like many writers and thinkers of his day, he was critical of religion, the Churches, and the clergy, but he was not disposed to take repressive action against any of them. Witticisms at their expense were quite in order, but that was all. As a matter of fact Gibbon was not so cold-blooded and anti-religious a sceptic as his detractors would have us believe. On the contrary, he was so deeply interested in religion that he could neither leave it alone nor rest satisfied with its conventional expressions as provided by the Churches. What he criticized and ridiculed, it should be noted, was not what he called 'pure' religion or 'pure' Christianity, but the Church with its priests and monks, its popes and saints, its miracles, and its absurd theological wrangles. Critics of *The Decline and Fall* have not ordinarily remarked that its author never spoke disrespectfully of Jesus[25] or described the primitive and uncorrupted Christianity to which he sometimes referred. In fact his nearest approach to an account of the life and teachings of Jesus is to be found in a few lines near the beginning of chapter xlvii in which Gibbon traced the historical development of the theological doctrine of the Incarnation.

> The familiar companions of Jesus of Nazareth conversed with their friend and countryman, who, in all the actions of rational and animal life, appeared of the same species with themselves. His progress from infancy to youth and manhood was marked by a regular increase in stature and wisdom; and after a painful agony of mind and body, he expired on the cross. He lived and died for the service of mankind; but the life and death of Socrates had likewise been devoted to the cause of religion and justice; and, although the stoic or the hero may disdain the humble virtues of Jesus, the tears which he shed over his friend and country may be esteemed the purest evidence of his humanity.[26]

No matter how beautiful this 'pure' Christianity may originally have been, it was soon corrupted, Gibbon asserted, by priestly avarice and lust for power, and this corrupt Christianity became a major factor in bringing about the fall of Rome. 'I have described the triumph of barbarism and religion', he declared near the end of

The Decline and Fall, and a few years later he wrote in his Memoirs: 'As I believed [in 1776], and as I still believe, that the propagation of the gospel and the triumph of the Church are inseparably connected with the decline of the Roman Monarchy, I weighed the causes and effects of the Revolution.' As this passage was probably written late in 1789, the word 'Revolution' suggests the events then transpiring in France. A few months later he became more specific in his comparison of early Christianity with revolutionary France. In a letter to Lord Sheffield, dated 5 February 1791, he spoke briefly but eloquently of the pleasure he derived from reading Edmund Burke's intemperate *Reflections on the French Revolution*, after which he continued, in the next sentence: 'The primitive Church, which I have treated with some freedom, was itself at that time, an innovation, and *I* was attached to the old Pagan establishment.'[27]

All was not loss, however, for the spirit of liberty managed somehow to survive the darkness of the Middle Ages, and at the close of a chapter on medieval heresy Gibbon declared that, in spite of their bigotry, the Protestant Reformers promoted liberty by their divisions, since no one faction could suppress all the others. 'The names of Zwinglius, Luther, and Calvin are pronounced with gratitude as the deliverers of nations.' Continuing the story down to his own day, Gibbon points out that 'the free governments of Holland and England introduce the practice of toleration', and that 'the volumes of controversy are overspread with cobwebs; the doctrine of a Protestant church is far removed from the knowledge or belief of its private members; and the forms of orthodoxy, the articles of faith, are subscribed with a sigh or a smile by the modern clergy'.[28]

Further light is thrown upon Gibbon's religious views by an examination of his relations with his Aunt Hester. Hester Gibbon had not lived on amicable terms with her brother, for she was scandalized by his intimacy with the infidel Mallet, and he resented her receiving a large share of their father's estate; but the historian took no part in these family quarrels, and he saw little of his aunt. A few weeks after returning from his first stay in Lausanne he wrote her a stiff and formal letter (apparently with his tongue in his cheek) announcing his safe arrival in England, assuring her that he was fully disabused of his 'unhappy ideas' (Catholicism), expressing regret that he had never enjoyed the happiness of profiting by her precepts and example, and soliciting her friendship. Gibbon heard little more from her until 1770, when she wrote him 'a very odd' letter, now lost, on the occasion of his father's death. During the next few years she annoyed him by calling upon him for his aid in various business transactions and even trying (in vain) to borrow money from him. In letters to Holroyd he often referred to her sarcastically as 'the Saint'; by way of contrast he sometimes called himself 'the Atheist'; and he once declared it 'possible enough' that she was a hypocrite.[29]

On her rare visits to London she notified him of her arrival and allowed him to visit her at her lodgings, but she firmly refused to set foot in his house. After one of these visits, in 1774, Gibbon permitted himself a little fun at her expense. 'She is in truth a very great curiosity', he wrote to his stepmother; 'her dress and figure exceed every thing we had in the Masquerade. Her language and ideas belong to the last century. However in point of religion she was rational, that is to say silent.'[30] Gibbon might laugh, but he put up with his aunt's demands, partly for family reasons, no doubt, but partly perhaps because he, being her closest relative, had good reason to expect that she would name him as her heir. He did not count very much on the legacy, however, for he admitted to his stepmother, in the letter just cited, that 'In the light of interest, however, her regard is of little consequence to me; if I may judge from her appearance her life is a better one than mine.' Thus expecting her to outlive him, he did not build up his hopes, and he was not greatly distressed when his aunt finally died (1790), at the age of eighty-four, and left most of her property to the family of William Law.

Various passages in Gibbon's letters to his Aunt Hester have led to speculation about a possible change of his views on religion in his later years. The most important of these passages occurs in a letter of 1788: 'Whatever you may have been told of my opinions, I can assure you with truth that I consider Religion as the best guide to youth and the best support of old age: that I firmly believe that there is less real happiness in the business and pleasures of the World, than in the life, which you have chosen, of devotion and retirement.'[31] Some critics regard this passage as evidence that, when he wrote it, Gibbon was on the verge of returning to the religion of his childhood, but others remind us that 'a man is not on his oath when he writes to his aunt'. Each of these suggestions contains a measure of truth, no doubt, yet neither, by itself, is wholly satisfactory. The most that we can say is that at this time Gibbon was still thinking seriously about religious matters.

There certainly was no need for Gibbon to write lies to his aunt, but if he was not deliberately lying to her, and if this letter expresses his opinions accurately, why did he so regularly spice the footnotes to his History with slurs and attacks upon the early Christians, and why did he make religious recluses like his aunt an especial butt of his wit? Here again Porson's famous criticism of Gibbon may help us. 'He often makes, when he cannot readily find, an occasion to insult our religion; which he hates so cordially that he might seem to revenge some personal injury.'[32] 'Hates' is too strong a word, but as to the personal injury there can be no doubt: Gibbon's life had been disrupted for years by his conversion to Rome, and he carried the scars ever after. In attacking the Church, however, Gibbon was actuated not by a desire to avenge these sufferings, but by fear — fear that he might again do something impulsive if he let himself go.

Like other members of his family Gibbon was a man capable of religious feeling. He was no William Law, no Hester Gibbon, but after the misfortune of his momentary conversion to Rome and the spectacle of his Aunt Hester, he trembled at the thought of giving way to religious emotions. He therefore disciplined himself rigorously, adopting a coldly rationalistic attitude towards life and building up the picture of Christianity that we find in his History. The general pattern of his anticlericalism therefore resembles that of his conduct towards Suzanne Curchod during his second stay at Lausanne; he knew that he could never marry her, much as he might desire it, but he found that he could not forget her or even keep away from her; he therefore accused her (falsely) of various delinquencies in order to convince himself that she was unworthy of him; but after she was safely married to M. Necker he quickly forgot her alleged shortcomings and gladly accepted her as a dear and lifelong friend. He put on the same defensive armour against the Church, though fortifying his denunciations with wit rather than with indignation: he never made jokes at Suzanne's expense, and only rarely was he really indignant with the early Christians.

Gibbon had expected that his treatment of Christianity would trouble some readers, but he was sincerely surprised at the uproar that followed the publication of his first volume. He could not believe that educated Englishmen were 'so fondly attached to the name and shadow of Christianity', and he assures us in his Memoirs that 'had I foreseen that the pious, the timid, and the prudent would feel, or affect to feel, with such exquisite sensibility, I might perhaps have softened the two invidious Chapters, which would create many enemies and conciliate few friends'.[33] Confirmation of this assurance is to be found in a note which Lord Sheffield prepared for his edition of the Memoirs but did not use. 'Some time after the attack on the 15th and 16th Chapters had commenced, he ... asked whether I thought it advisable to withdraw the offensive passages in the second Edition, then at the Press.'[34] Sheffield had no difficulty in persuading Gibbon not to omit these passages, but the fact that Gibbon had even considered such a mutilation of his book is highly significant. Would he have suggested it if he regarded Christianity as a major cause of the decline and fall of Rome? If, on the other hand, Gibbon conducted his researches and wrote these passages primarily to convince himself, it would make less difference whether they appeared in the book or not. They had fulfilled their purpose when they persuaded their author.

Gibbon mellowed greatly after making Lausanne his permanent residence in 1783, but the outbreak of the French Revolution disturbed his new-found equanimity, and it broke down the defences that he had so laboriously built up to ward off the dangers of excessive religion. The venomous language that he used against the French equalled or surpassed anything that he had ever said about the early Christians. Sometimes he used the same words against his new enemies, 'fanatic' being the chief of them.

In these troubled times, therefore, Gibbon's scepticism broke down, but the thoughts that now rose to the surface of his mind were not new thoughts. All his life they had been struggling for recognition, but he had usually managed to keep them buried in the darker corners of his mind. One of these thoughts might occasionally rise to the surface, as when he praised his aunt's way of life, but he soon managed to force it back into its dungeon.

At bottom Gibbon was a religious man, raised in a religious family under the influence of William Law, and, struggle as he would, he could not live down this legacy of the past. It is a significant fact that while superficial religionists damned his book and its author, some of his most enthusiastic admirers have been religious leaders who deplored his witticisms at the expense of the Christians, but who recognized that he had something to tell them. The editor of the standard nineteenth-century edition of Gibbon's History was H. H. Milman, Dean of St. Paul's in London; and when the famous John Henry Newman (who had read Gibbon enthusiastically as an undergraduate and who cited him frequently) was about to forsake the Anglican communion he wrote, in his last Anglican book: 'It is melancholy to say it, but the chief, perhaps the only English writer who has any claim to be considered an ecclesiastical historian, is the unbeliever Gibbon.'[35]

CHAPTER FIVE

'MY CURSED POLITICAL LIFE'

GIBBON'S biographers usually are so fascinated by their hero's love affair with Suzanne Curchod, his adventures in religion, and the stories of his prodigious reading that they leave themselves little time to examine his political ideas and activities. The blame for this neglect of an important aspect of his career may be attributed in large measure to Gibbon himself. Because his political activities ended in disaster, he skipped over them as lightly as possible in his Memoirs, and later biographers have followed the pattern thus set. Gibbon was neither original nor profound as a political thinker, yet his understanding — or perhaps his misunderstanding — of the government of eighteenth-century England played a significant part in shaping his theories about the decline and fall of ancient Rome. We must therefore describe his political education, trace the unhappy course of his parliamentary career, and examine his views on the major political issues of his day.

James II had been driven from the English throne by the 'Glorious Revolution' of 1688, but for many years the historian's great-grandfather, Matthew Gibbon, remained a Jacobite, loyal to the Stuart dynasty. At first Matthew's son, the first Edward Gibbon, shared his father's sympathies, but financial prosperity eventually mellowed his Jacobitism into mere Toryism, and in the last days of Queen Anne (1710–14) he sat on the Board of Customs. His grandson informs us that he concealed his Jacobite opinions except for a few harmless toasts, but that in the daily devotions of the family the name of the king for whom they prayed was prudently omitted. The elder Gibbon's latent Jacobitism and his misfortunes at the time of the 'South Sea Bubble' made it doubly difficult for him to accept the Hanoverian kings, and he was disqualified from all public trust.[1] Seventy years later his grandson still regarded this disqualification as a major and most unjust part of his punishment: a man of his abilities, the grandson believed, should have occupied a seat in Parliament and perhaps have held other important government posts as well.

The second Edward Gibbon was not a man to attach himself openly to so hopelessly lost a cause as Jacobitism. In the days of George II he sat as a Tory in two parliaments where, according to his son's report, he quietly maintained his father's hostility to the Whig ministry. 'In the opposition to Sir Robert Walpole and the Pelhams, he was connected with the Tories — shall I say the Jacobites? With them he gave many a vote, with them he drank many a bottle. But the prejudices of youth were gradually corrected by time, temper, and good sense.' Nevertheless his standing among loyalists was so recent and so open to question that, when the Young Pretender invaded England in 1745, he felt obliged to dismiss his Jacobite chaplain when that unhappy man, reading prayers one day in the parish church, 'most unluckily forgot the name of King George'.[2]

The historian was eight years old in 1745, and he long remembered how he had been 'reviled and buffeted' by his schoolmates for the sins of his Tory ancestors. These buffetings did not convert him to the Whig cause, however, or even make him a pro-Hanoverian Tory (of whom there were many by this time), and his experiences at Oxford (where the 'constitutional toasts were not expressive of the most lively loyalty for the House of Hanover') probably strengthened his youthful Jacobitism. Gibbon tells us nothing of his political opinions at this period, but there is no reason to doubt that he was as staunch a Jacobite as any of the 'monks of Magdalen'. At any rate, soon after his arrival in Lausanne he informed Pavillard that he was a partisan of the Pretender. It therefore devolved upon the tutor to redeem his pupil from Jacobitism as well as from Catholicism. Apparently Pavillard accomplished this task without great difficulty, for we hear no more about the Pretender.[3]

After young Gibbon had been adequately purged of his unfortunate ideas, both Jacobite and Catholic, he began reading modern authors on political theory. Though he dipped into the writings of Grotius and Puffendorf, he found Locke and Montesquieu more to his taste. He made Locke's *Essay concerning Human Understanding* the subject of a correspondence with a Swiss clergyman, M. Allamand, of Bex, and at about this time he read the same author's *Treatises on Government*. Here Locke demolished the doctrine, so dear to Jacobites, of the divine right of kings, and set forth the Whig principles of government in classic form. Gibbon was even more impressed by Montesquieu's two famous works, *De l'Esprit des lois* and the *Considérations sur les causes de la grandeur des romains et de leur décadence*.[4]

Two of Gibbon's early writings show how well he had learned his lessons from these men. A brief essay, written in 1761, on 'The Title of Charles VIII to the Crown of Naples', concludes with a rather sententious affirmation of the Whig doctrine that 'the only title [to a crown] not liable to objection is the consenting voice of a free people'.[5] The second essay is even more significant. Written soon after Gibbon's return to Lausanne in 1763, it is a twenty-page attack upon Berne's rule over the Vaud area, Lausanne and the surrounding territory. For more than two centuries this region had been ruled by emissaries from Berne, while Berne itself was ruled by a hereditary clique drawn from a few noble families. Though Berne's rule over Vaud was mild, and the Vaudois were not dissatisfied, Gibbon found much to criticize. In imitation, perhaps, of Montesquieu's *Lettres persanes*, he gave his essay the form of a letter from a Swedish traveller to a Swiss friend. After a few complimentary remarks on the beauty of life in Vaud, the youthful author fell to work deploring the lack of liberty there and stating categorically that 'deprived of liberty, you lack everything'. A page or two later he declared that 'If Liberty consists in being subject only to laws whose object is the welfare of the community, you are not free.' Gibbon then proceeded to point out many ways in which the Bernese aristocracy exploited the Vaudois, and even voiced the opinion that this exploitation was the real cause of Lausanne's cultural backwardness. Though he wrote disparagingly of the 'general will', of which Rousseau was then saying so much, he showed a high regard for Montesquieu's political and sociological theories. After levelling these severe criticisms against the Bernese rule of Vaud, Gibbon terminated his essay in a manner that was almost insulting to the Vaudois, sadly (but falsely) prophesying that they would never make an effort to regain their lost liberty.[6]

Why did Gibbon express these pessimistic views about the Vaudois, of whom he ordinarily held so high an opinion, and why was he so critical of the Bernese government? Before we can answer these questions we must examine the circumstances under which the letter was written. Unfortunately the manuscript bears no date, but probably it was written in the summer of 1763, soon after Gibbon's second arrival in Lausanne. On a night in June of that year Gibbon and some of his English friends drank too much wine and created such a disturbance that the police intervened and the offenders were taken to the local court. According to the police records a 'M. Guibbon' was spokesman for the Englishmen — probably because he was the only member of the party able to speak French fluently. The case dragged slowly through the court, but by standing firm and threatening an appeal to Berne, Gibbon saved his friends from punishment and even induced the officials to reprimand a police officer who had threatened them with his bayonet. This episode may have inspired Gibbon's letter on the government of Berne. The Lausanne police had offended his dignity, but they had also shown him the awe in which officials of Vaud held the authorities at Berne. By accusing the Vaudois of slavishness, and by citing instances of the tyranny to which they pusillanimously subjected themselves, Gibbon relieved his injured pride, after which he promptly forgot the whole affair.[7]

Gibbon's essay is rather trivial, yet it is important to anyone studying the development of his political ideas, and its subsequent history is most interesting. No matter when or why he wrote it, the essay shows that Gibbon had wandered far from his ancestral Jacobitism and Toryism. The author of this essay was a full-blown Whig, voicing the ideas of 1688. Moreover, the essay has been hailed as a document of importance in the history of Switzerland. Gibbon probably showed it to no one at the time he wrote it, and for thirty years it lay among his papers, unnoticed and forgotten. Lord Sheffield published it among Gibbon's letters in 1796, but as it was only one letter among more than two hundred, and was buried in the middle of a large and rather forbidding quarto volume, it at first attracted no attention. Two years later, however, an English lady (Miss Helen Maria Williams) published *A Tour in Switzerland*, in which she incorporated most of Gibbon's essay, and her book was at once translated into French. Revolutionary ideas about liberty were by this time sweeping over Switzerland from France, and in 1798 Vaudois agitators took a leading part in establishing the 'Helvetian Republic' under French protection — in spite of Gibbon's gloomy prediction that the people of Lausanne would never revolt. The rule of the Bernese aristocracy collapsed, and Vaud has ever since been an autonomous canton in the Swiss confederation. Gibbon would have been horrified had he foreseen what was going to happen, but several persons favouring the new régime reprinted his essay, at least in part, using it to justify what they were doing. Gibbon was thus made to provide an ideological foundation for their liberal reform, and his admirers may justly claim for him a place — although a small one, and an involuntary one at that — among the fathers of modern Swiss liberty.

In the year 1719, when at the height of his success as a business-man and financier, the first Edward Gibbon had decided that he would like to sit in Parliament and, with this end in view, he bought 'a weighty share' in the borough of Petersfield. (Before the reforms of 1832 this town, lying about five miles from Buriton, was a 'pocket borough' of 'burgage tenure' from which a handful of electors sent two members to the House of Commons.) Before he could make use of his purchase, however, the 'South Sea Bubble' burst and, as his grandson lamented, he was disqualified from all public trust. Fourteen years later, in 1734, the electors of Petersfield sent the second Edward Gibbon to Parliament, but in 1739 he sold his interest in the borough to his colleague and rival, Sir William Jolliffe. Though the historian wondered, in his Memoirs, why his father alienated so important a property, we may safely assume that he did so because of his chronic financial embarrassments. At the next general election (1741) he was elected to Parliament for Southampton — after the Tory authorities had arbitrarily created 170 new freemen to vote for him. After the dissolution of this parliament in 1747 the second Edward Gibbon never sought public office again, but he set his heart on some day seeing his son in Parliament.[8]

A few weeks after young Gibbon's return from Lausanne in 1758 his father discussed a parliamentary career with him, offering to provide the £1500 required to 'buy' him a seat in that body. Gibbon admitted to being tempted by his father's proposal, and for a moment he dreamed that he might 'shine in so august an assembly', or might even be 'the instrument of some good to my country', but nothing was settled at this time.[9] Father and son continued their interest in politics, however, and when a parliamentary by-election was held in their county of Hampshire (November 1759) the elder Gibbon contributed £100, the younger £25 (his total income for one month) to one of the candidates — who nevertheless was not elected.

The elder Gibbon again brought up the matter of a parliamentary seat in the spring of 1760, and again his son refused to commit himself. Though he was then staying with his father at Buriton,

Buriton Manor House today

and seeing him every day, young Gibbon wrote him a long and careful letter declaring himself not fitted for a parliamentary career (he certainly was not) and asking permission to use the £1500 for a year or two in Lausanne and Italy. Again nothing was decided.[10]

At the time of the general election of 1761 Gibbon's father made one final attempt to push his son into Parliament. When a number of freeholders in Petersfield requested him to stand against Jolliffe, he suggested that they transfer their votes to his son. They agreed, and the son accepted their offer. He did a little canvassing, but within a week he withdrew from the contest because Jolliffe had won over some of his important partisans. In his Memoirs Gibbon made no mention of this disappointing affair, and in his Journal he merely noted that the experience 'cost hardly anything' and that he 'withdrew with honour'.[11] It is very probable, however, that his pride was wounded more deeply than he chose to admit. His speech of withdrawal was quite bitter, and he never forgave Jolliffe. The two men maintained civil relations with each other, even exchanging dinners occasionally, but Gibbon spoke severely of his rival in letters to his stepmother, sarcastically referring to him as 'Lord Petersfield' and once, more than ten years later, he exclaimed, 'What a fool, what a great fool, what an egregious fool he is!'

During the next several years Gibbon's time was fully occupied with the militia (he did not resign his commission until 1770), his travels, his studies, the distractions arising from his father's long illness and death (1770), and various public duties forced upon him by his position as lord of the manor at Buriton. In 1768 he became a Justice of the Peace, whose task it was to preside over the manorial court twice a year, trying petty civil and criminal cases. He disliked this duty intensely, and, like many of his fellow Justices in those days, he hired an attorney from Petersfield to hold court for him. But unlike most of his fellow Justices, he took his position seriously enough to read Blackstone through three times — a formidable task.

Meantime Gibbon had not forgotten Parliament. When in

London he enjoyed listening to the debates in the House of Commons, and his letters of this period, especially those to Holroyd, are full of political news and gossip. When the Buriton estate had been leased, and he was safely installed in his London house, he began to think more seriously of entering Parliament. He apparently discussed the matter with his stepmother and with Holroyd, both of whom encouraged him, and it presently occurred to them that his kinsman by marriage, Edward Eliot, might be the means of accomplishing their design.*

We do not know when or how Eliot first became acquainted with the Gibbon family, but in 1753, when young Gibbon announced his conversion to Roman Catholicism, it was Eliot who suggested that the boy be sent to Lausanne for re-education. Three years later Eliot married Gibbon's cousin, Miss Katharine Elliston, daughter of the second Edward Gibbon's sister, Katharine, who allegedly was the model for the worldly sister in William Law's *Serious Call.* We are told that she brought her husband a dowry of more than £60,000. Gibbon's letters to his stepmother in 1771 mention the Eliots frequently, speaking of his 'amazing friendship' with them, telling how 'we are grown wonderfully intimate', and reporting that he and Eliot's sister were 'huge friends'. It was only natural, therefore, that when Gibbon wished to enter Parliament he should turn to Eliot for aid.

Gibbon proceeded with circumspection in his campaign. The

* Edward Eliot (1727–1804), a wealthy Cornish landowner, was entitled to nominate two Members of Parliament for St. Germans and two for Liskeard, and as, in Gibbon's neat phrase, 'the Electors of Liskeard are commonly of the same opinion as Mr. Eliot', nomination by him was tantamount to election. Since he also exercised a powerful influence in the borough of Grampound, Eliot controlled six seats in the House of Commons. Entering Parliament himself at the age of twenty-one, he occupied one or another of these seats until he was promoted to the House of Lords thirty-six years later (1784). He was then able to provide two of his three sons with seats in the House. One of these sons presently married the granddaughter of Lord Chancellor Hardwicke, and the other married the sister of the prime minister, William Pitt. These achievements show that Eliot was an eminently successful politician and social climber, but he is scarcely to be numbered among England's major statesmen.

year 1772 kept him busy finishing his business regarding Buriton and getting himself established in his London house, but early in 1773 he and his stepmother began planning to visit Port Eliot — the Eliots' residence in Cornwall, near St. Germans. In one of his letters to Mrs. Gibbon he called Eliot 'the Lord of Boroughs' — which indicates the main reason for their proposed visit. While at Port Eliot in September Gibbon wrote to Holroyd that Eliot lacked many things, notably a library, but 'one possession he has indeed most truly desirable [i.e. a parliamentary seat]; but I much fear that the Danae of St. Germains has no particular inclination for me and that the interested Strumpet will yield only to a Golden Shower. My situation is the more perplexing as I cannot with any degree of delicacy make the first advances.'[12]

The Eliots are mentioned occasionally in Gibbon's correspondence during the next several months, but he wrote nothing of his parliamentary ambitions. Then, on 10 September 1774, he announced 'great things' to Holroyd: Eliot had 'at last' promised him an 'independent' seat in Parliament.* Two weeks later, on 24 September Gibbon's Aunt Kitty wrote a most interesting letter to his stepmother. 'Although you have had a very satisfactory account of Mr. Gibbon from himself, I take the first opportunity to rejoice with you upon the prospect of our friend making a figure in Parliament. I own I flatter myself as I am sure you do. I only fear

* There were, of course, financial transactions connected with Gibbon's seat in Parliament. Eliot gave Gibbon his seat at a bargain price (£1200), which Gibbon was to pay eight years later, but which he apparently never paid at all. In 1761 Eliot had charged £2000 for a seat, and by 1780 his price had risen to £3000, following a nation-wide trend. Part of the money thus collected was used to win over voters by various means, part was profit for the 'owner' of the borough. Eliot did not wholly approve of this system, but he used it successfully. As late as 1797 he wrote to Pitt, then the prime minister: 'In election transactions I have never received what in the one town or the other I had not previously laid out. Such receipts were matters of necessity — I have never submitted to them without a feeling of reluctance. Often I have received nothing, and not infrequently have thereby suffered very considerable inconvenience.' See Namier and Brooke, *The History of Parliament* (art. 'Eliot, Edward'), II, 382.

I shall not live to see it, in short it is the only thing in the world I am anxious about. Why it was not done sooner and several other things upon that subject I defer until I have the pleasure of seeing you.' These cryptic remarks seem to indicate that the two ladies had a larger share in getting Gibbon into Parliament than has usually been suspected.[13]

Parliament was unexpectedly dissolved on 30 September 1774, several months before its term was out, and new elections were held at once. On 14 October Gibbon was able to notify his stepmother and Holroyd that he had been elected as the Member for Liskeard.

Gibbon's letters of the next few months bear witness to the pleasure and high enthusiasm with which he entered Parliament. In spite of his earlier remarks about being unfitted for a political career and his later bitterness about his 'cursed political life', he was delighted when Eliot finally made him the offer for which he and his friends had so long been angling. In his early enthusiasm Gibbon wrote to his stepmother that Eliot's offer 'changes the colour of my whole future life', and six months later he told her that his parliamentary duties had made 'an agreeable improvement' in his life for they provided 'just the mixture of business, of study, and of society which I have always imagined I should, and now find I do like'.[14]

In his early days Gibbon had occasionally referred to himself as a Whig, but that name then meant little. The group of politicians once held together by Walpole, Newcastle, the Pelhams, and Chatham had split into factions, no one of which could maintain an ascendancy in Parliament. Everyone now accepted the Hanoverian dynasty and the fundamental Whig doctrines of 1688, and the old terms 'Whig' and 'Tory' were falling into desuetude. The important question was whether a man voted with the ministry or against it. During the 1760s one unstable ministry followed another, but in 1770 Lord North became prime minister, in spite of bitter criticism by such men as Rockingham, Shelburne, Fox, and Burke, and he remained in office for twelve years.

The new Parliament assembled on 29 November 1774, and its first business, of course, was to approve an address to the throne. Gibbon voted with the ministry and reported to Holroyd that, though he had been sorely tempted to speak, he had kept silent during the debate. This desire to address Parliament on his first day in office indicates the zeal with which he entered upon his political career, but his failure to speak is even more significant. During the next few weeks he often apologized to friends for his continued silence. 'The great speakers fill me with despair,' he explained, 'the bad ones with terror.' This initial reaction to parliamentary oratory set up a block in Gibbon's mind which he could not overcome. Throughout his nine years in Parliament he remained frustrated and silent.

The most colourful of the early critics of the Government was the notorious demagogue, John Wilkes, who had stood for Parliament in Middlesex in 1768 and, after a turbulent campaign, had been elected by a four-to-one majority. Early in 1769, however, the Commons expelled him because of his demagogic activities. The populace of London rushed to his defence with the cry, 'Wilkes and Liberty', and presently he was elected Lord Mayor of London. In 1774 he was again elected to Parliament, and as soon as he had taken his seat he began demanding that the parliamentary resolutions of 1769 against him be expunged from the record. Many members of the Opposition supported Wilkes, for political reasons, but his motion was voted down. Not until 1782, after Wilkes's day of glory had departed, were the resolutions quashed.

Gibbon had met Wilkes while in the militia and found him a most interesting companion. He was more than a little shocked, however, by the man's blasphemous and bawdy conversation, and he commented in his Journal that 'shame is a weakness he has long since surmounted'. The two men did not meet again until both were in Parliament, but on the day Wilkes's motion was discussed in the Commons (22 February 1775) Gibbon 'sat beside the Lord Mayor' and voted as a 'Patriot' — that is, with Wilkes against North. It is not clear why Gibbon voted as he did (he certainly had no sympathy with Wilkes's political activities), but his vote attracted attention, and he expressed relief when he learned that his 'constituents' (i.e. Eliot) approved his action.[15] Moreover, friends of the Administration were convinced that something should be done to assure themselves of this new member's support in the future. Towards the middle of April Gibbon was invited to dine with Lord North, and a few days later he was presented at court.

The most important problems then facing the British Government concerned the American colonies, which rose in armed rebellion in 1775. George III and North believed that the rebels could and should be brought to heel by military force, and at first their views prevailed in Parliament. After Burgoyne's surrender at Saratoga (17 October 1777), however, the Opposition steadily gained strength. At last, in March 1782, North was replaced, first for a brief period by Rockingham, and then by Shelburne (July 1782–February 1783), who recognized American independence and made peace.

When Gibbon entered Parliament he was not well informed on American affairs. In his childhood he had read books about explorers and settlers, but he had given little attention to the political problems presented by the American colonies in his own day. After taking his seat in Parliament he undertook a more careful study of the question. He sought out and conversed with a certain Israel Mauduit, agent of the Massachusetts colony in London, and Thomas Hutchinson, the governor of Massachusetts who had recently been recalled. Each of these men disapproved of North's policies. Regarding Mauduit, Gibbon declared: 'He squeaks out a great deal of sense and knowledge, though after all I mean to think and perhaps to speak for myself.' Six weeks later, at the end of January 1775, Hutchinson reported that Gibbon was for 'supporting the authority of Parliament but ready to any reasonable concession'. But at about this time Gibbon reported to his stepmother, 'I have hitherto been a zealous though silent friend to the Cause of Government which *in this instance* [italics his], I think the Cause of England', and he wrote to Holroyd: 'I am more and more convinced that with firmness all may go well: yet I sometimes doubt Lord N.' But a few weeks later Hutchinson said of Gibbon: 'I think, in general, he will be in Opposition; dropped something like Lord Chatham's being a necessary man in such difficult cases.'[16] Gibbon obviously had not yet made up his mind about the American colonies, but he was thinking about them and, like a true scholar, he was able to see both sides of the question. Again like a scholar, he was unable to decide what should be done.

During the next few months Gibbon's letters often express concern over events in America, but in Parliament he continued to vote with the North ministry. These months were perhaps the busiest and happiest in his life, and he had much to do besides study the American question. He was putting the finishing touches on the manuscript of the first volume of *The Decline and Fall* (which was sent to the printer in June 1775); he entertained the Neckers when they visited London in the spring of 1776; and he was their guest in Paris from May to October 1777.

At the time of Gibbon's visit, Parisian society was enjoying a splurge of enthusiasm for Benjamin Franklin, who had recently arrived in France, seeking friendship and aid for his fellow countrymen in their struggle for independence. Gibbon dined with him on one occasion, though he insisted to Holroyd that it was purely by accident.[17] Nevertheless gossips enlarged upon this meeting and reported that when the British historian showed a certain coolness towards the American philosopher, the philosopher offered to present him with materials which he might find helpful when he came to write the decline and fall of the *British* Empire.

Better authenticated anecdotes about Gibbon also went the rounds in Paris. One such story told of an encounter with the formidable Abbé de Mably, in which the historian defended the English form of monarchical government while the Abbé urged the merits of republicanism: the discussion became acrimonious, and Gibbon was getting decidedly the best of it, when their host separated the disputants. Others told of a battle royal between Gibbon and the Duke of Richmond over the American question. The duke, who was highly critical of Lord North and his policies, had been a friend and neighbour of the historian's father and a student at Westminster with Gibbon himself. Gibbon admitted to having met him socially almost every day when he was in Paris, and conceded that there had been 'a few slight skirmishes', but he strenuously denied anything that 'deserves the name of a general engagement'. He went on to remark, however, that he found it 'much easier to defend the justice than the policy of our Measures; but there are cases where whatever is repugnant to sound policy ceases to be just'.[18] Gibbon's experiences in Paris undoubtedly influenced his thinking regarding the American war, though he refused to admit it even to himself. He was not the man to seek applause by criticizing his country before foreigners, or to permit others to do so unrebuked, but the fact that the French were lionizing him made it doubly easy for him to be impressed by what they said.

When Parliament convened on 20 November 1777, shortly after Gibbon's return from France, he noticed 'a universal desire of peace, even on the most humble conditions', and he declared that 'if it were not for shame, there were not twenty men in the House who were not ready to vote for peace'.[19] Early in December, when news reached London of General Burgoyne's surrender at Saratoga, a general cry for peace led to the warmest debates in Parliament that Gibbon remembered hearing. He had recently written to Holroyd asking him — a trifle condescendingly, it seems — 'Are you still fierce?'; a week later, after he had heard the 'dreadful' news of Saratoga, he warned his friend that 'you will find youself obliged to carry on this glorious War almost alone'; and on 16 December he assured his stepmother: 'I shall scarcely give my consent to exhaust still farther the finest country in the World in the prosecution of a War, from whence no reasonable man entertains any hopes of success. It is better to be humbled than ruined.' In general he shared the view of those who held that 'after the substance of power was lost, the name of independence might be granted to the Americans'.[20]

Saratoga thus brought Gibbon close to the parliamentary Opposition, and especially to Charles James Fox. Gibbon had known Fox for several years. Both men belonged to Brooks's Club, then much frequented by Whig politicians, and here Gibbon listened night after night to Fox declaiming on America. In the early weeks of 1778 the two men saw each other more frequently than ever, and presently Gibbon, too, began to declaim against Lord North and his policies. On 27 January and again on 2 February 1778 he voted with Fox against major Bills presented by the North ministry, and a few days later he wrote to Holroyd that, in his opinion, 'Lord North does not deserve pardon for the past, applause for the present, or confidence for the future.'[21]

Burgoyne's surrender convinced the French Government that a little aid would enable the Americans to gain their independence, thereby inflicting a shattering blow upon the British Empire. They therefore concluded a commercial treaty and an alliance with the rebellious Americans (6 February 1778), but at first they limited their aid to supplying their new allies with munitions, lending them money, and allowing their privateers to use French ports. Diplomatic relations between England and France were severed late in March, and the first naval engagement came in May. By this time Lord North had announced (17 February) a new and more conciliatory policy towards the colonies. It was too late to appease the American rebels, but the French war, the national emergency, and the new policy brought Gibbon back into the Government fold. He was still highly dissatisfied with the way the war was being conducted, but he could do nothing except wring his hands, complain at Brooks's, and think and write about the decline of ancient Rome.

Gibbon's financial troubles had not ceased with the settlement of his father's estate for he believed that, being a 'Senator' as well as a gentleman and a scholar, he must cut a fine figure in London society. Like his father before him he lived beyond his means, eating up his capital, and even failing to pay his stepmother all that was due her. He regularly and promptly remitted the £200 a year due her from the estate at Buriton, but he did not pay the £100 interest he owed on a personal note that she held. When she found it difficult to make ends meet on this scanty income, she talked of taking cheaper quarters at Bath and even of retiring to a village in Essex, while Gibbon, in his turn, began talking about a return to Lausanne, where living would be cheaper than in London.[22] He also began looking for additional income, however, and early in 1779 he was able to assure his stepmother that a powerful friend would presently help him. Six months elapsed before this friend (Alexander Wedderburn, later Lord Loughborough, attorney-general in North's cabinet) was able to find a place for him, but at last, on 2 July 1779, Gibbon was appointed one of the lords commissioners of trade and plantations at a salary of £1000 a year, or about £750 after taxes.* Gibbon's financial difficulties were eased; he paid his stepmother the £100 interest promptly thereafter; and he continued to live in London in the style to which he had become accustomed.[23]

Two weeks before Gibbon was notified of his appointment to the Board of Trade, Spain had declared war on England (16 June 1779), charging the British with a variety of misdeeds. Lord Weymouth, secretary of state for the northern and southern departments, answered these charges, but before publishing his reply

* The duties of a commissioner of trade were not onerous, but it is quite incorrect to speak of Gibbon's place as a sinecure. During his three years in office the Board of Trade held 150 meetings, of which Gibbon attended 117 — or about four out of five. He was more regular in attendance than any other member except the president (Lord Grantham), who was present at all but one of the meetings held during his term of office. Edward Eliot, who had been a member of the board from 1760 to 1776, attended only 331 meetings out of 1250, less than one in three. (A. H. Basye, *The Lords Commissioners of Trade and Plantations* (1925), app. A, 224–9.)

he requested Gibbon to examine its French text and improve its literary style. A few days later, when the French Government issued a manifesto against the British (22 July), Weymouth asked the historian to prepare the official reply.[24] Gibbon was delighted with this commission, and in a thirty-page *Mémoire justificatif* he ably set forth England's complaints against France. When this memoir was published (in October 1779) it attracted wide attention at once; prominent persons spoke highly of it; and Gibbon boasted to Holroyd that it had even been translated into Turkish.

Meantime England's position in the world was steadily sinking. Her American colonies were virtually lost; France and Spain were waging war upon her; and Ireland was on the verge of revolt. On 11 June 1779 a member of the Opposition (William Meredith) moved in Parliament that the ministry be directed to 'immediately deliberate upon, and concert, such measures as may prepare the way for peace with America'. This motion was defeated without a division, but it expressed the desire of many Englishmen inside and outside Parliament. A few weeks later many high officials in England were in a panic from fear of a large-scale invasion of their island by the French, and on 4 September the secretary at war (Charles Jenkinson) wrote: 'I believe this country was never in so perilous a situation as it is at present, and the Events of the next fortnight will probably be as important as ever were known in History.'

The leaders of the parliamentary Opposition then decided that the time had come for them to redouble their attacks upon Lord North. Debates in Parliament became more bitter, and in the following spring North's enemies brought forward a series of measures designed to accomplish his downfall. First, in February 1780, Burke laid before Parliament an 'Economical Reform Bill', which would limit North's power of patronage by abolishing a large number of sinecure posts; the Bill was debated acrimoniously, but it was withdrawn before it came to a final vote. Then, on 6 April 1780, a member of the Opposition (John Dunning) moved a resolution boldly stating that 'the influence of the Crown has increased, is increasing, and ought to be diminished'. The House of Commons passed this resolution by a vote of 233 to 215. And finally, early in June 1780, Lord George Gordon (an eccentric, if not actually insane M.P.) added anti-Catholic agitation to the tumult, and London became the scene of bloody riots. These disturbances frightened so many people that North was again able to control Parliament, and the Commons rejected any steps to implement Dunning's resolution.

Gibbon had no desire to take an active part in these disputes, but he could not avoid expressing his opinions in the clubs if not in Parliament. Several leaders of the Opposition had been among his closest friends, and he had often expressed views very similar to theirs. They therefore turned upon him bitterly when he accepted a lucrative place under Lord North. Charles Fox attacked him severely on the floor of the House of Commons, enlivened the controversy with doggerel verses, and even asserted that one evening he heard Gibbon declare at Brooks's that 'there was no salvation for this country until six heads of the principal persons in Administration were laid on the table. Eleven days after this same gentleman accepted a place of Lord of Trade under these very Ministers, and has acted with them ever since.' Gibbon, or his friends, later modified this story, asserting that he said, 'until both North's and Fox's heads were on the table'. Perhaps Gibbon really did make some such remark about North, and perhaps he later expanded it to include Fox.[25]

Under the inspiration of these leaders the general public took up the hue and cry, and before long Gibbon was being assailed from every side. Strange as it may seem, his patriotic service in writing the *Mémoire justificatif* became an important item in the controversy and contributed signally to its author's ruin. Though this memoir had been published anonymously, the secret of its authorship was soon divulged, and Gibbon's enemies made haste to denounce the author and all his works. Wilkes charged that Gibbon had been given a sinecure on the Board of Trade as payment for deserting his friends and writing the memoir; other critics denounced the memoir as incompetent; and still others tried their hands at ridicule, with the London *Public Advertiser* taking the lead. One contributor to this radical journal lampooned Gibbon as 'Mr. Chubby Chub' in a series of scurrilous verses, while another quoted extracts from the first volume of *The Decline and Fall*, applying to Gibbon himself the various vices with which the historian had charged the Roman emperors and senators in the days of their decline.[26]

Though Gibbon pretended to ignore these personal attacks, his letters to his stepmother show how keenly he felt them. He lost whatever illusions he may once have entertained about the glory and prestige emanating from a seat in Parliament, and he repeatedly declared himself heartily sick of the whole business.[27] Four years later he was still writing to Holroyd about his 'cursed political life', but in his Memoirs he simply stated that 'My acceptance of a place provoked some of the Leaders of opposition, with whom I lived in habits of intimacy, and I was most unjustly accused of deserting a party in which I had never enlisted.'[28]

These attacks upon Gibbon continued throughout the year, and in the end they cost him his seat in Parliament, for when elections were held in September 1780, his 'great Constituent' refused to support him. Eliot was by this time so deeply engaged in the measures of the Opposition that his whole political future depended upon their success. Unfortunately, however, he was not able to deliver the votes of the Members of Parliament who owed their seats to him. Only one of Eliot's five members voted with him in favour of Dunning's famous resolution, while Gibbon and Eliot's other three members voted against it.[29] This independence at so critical a moment could not be tolerated, and when elections were ordered a few months later, the only loyal member was duly nominated and re-elected, while Eliot's four other members were unceremoniously cast off.

As early as May, Gibbon had suspected that something of the

sort might be in the cards, but he knew nothing definite until Eliot gave him the bad news early in August, barely three weeks before the new election. Gibbon then addressed a letter to his patron, complaining of his long silence and declaring that if he were not re-elected he must leave the country. Eliot replied that 'all circumstances being taken in and impartially weighed, I had no Idea that you either would or could have applied to me for a seat in the house of Commons'. He then stated that Gibbon's constituents in Liskeard were 'decidedly against choosing you again', and suggested that he apply to his new friends in the Government for aid. They would surely be able and happy to do something for so distinguished a person as the great Gibbon.[30]

Eliot was correct in assuring his cousin that North and Wedderburn would look after him, and on 7 September Gibbon wrote to Holroyd that, thanks to Lord North, 'I shall again breathe the pestiferous air of St. Stephen's Chappel.' Not until ten months later, however, was he elected member for Lymington in Hampshire (June 1781). This 'election' cost £3000, of which Gibbon paid £800, while the balance came from the king's account. This payment of £800 was a heavy drain on Gibbon's finances, but he must have a seat in Parliament if he was to retain his place on the Board of Trade and its salary of £750.[31]

Within a year another blow fell, which eventually deprived him of his place and its salary. Burke's 'Economical Reform Bill' (mentioned above) had been laid before the House of Commons in February 1780. The alleged purpose of this Bill was to effect economies in government by abolishing a large number of offices, but it soon appeared that its author intended to eliminate only those sinecures that were then enjoyed by friends of Lord North.* The Board of Trade stood second on his list of sinecures to be abolished,

* It was even suggested that he salvaged the second-richest sinecure in the kingdom (the clerkship of the pells, worth £7000 a year) because he hoped to get this office himself! 'Can one but smile', remarked Horace Walpole in his *Journal* (II, 556), 'at a reformer of abuses reserving the second greatest abuse for himself?'

and Burke was especially eloquent in his attacks upon it, calling it (as reported by Horace Walpole) 'a nest of crows with one nightingale in it'. This one nightingale may perhaps have been Gibbon, but even if so, Burke did not spare him. In the course of his attack upon the Board of Trade, he commented with heavy sarcasm on 'the historian's labours, the wise and salutary result of deep religious researches'.[32] When the Commons took up the Bill, clause by clause, they voted 207 to 199 in favour of abolishing the Board of Trade, but as the debate proceeded they rejected so many clauses that the whole Bill was withdrawn. Gibbon's place was saved for a moment, but as soon as the North ministry fell (20 March 1782) a slightly revised Reform Bill was prepared. On 11 July this Bill became law, and the Board of Trade was abolished. Gibbon was left with nothing but a parliamentary seat which he no longer wanted. He tried to sell this seat (such a transaction was not impossible in eighteenth-century England), but before a purchaser could be found, Parliament was dissolved and Gibbon found himself with nothing left to sell.

In spite of these disasters Gibbon attempted to maintain a philosophic calm, and in 1783, when things were at their worst, he wrote some of the most justly famous chapters of *The Decline and Fall.* Nevertheless his reaction to a letter from Dr. Joseph Priestley showed how deeply his troubles were disturbing him. Priestley is remembered today primarily as the chemist who discovered oxygen, but he was also a Unitarian minister in Birmingham and he wrote copiously on theological topics. In 1782 he set forth his views in a two-volume *History of the Corruptions of Christianity*, copies of which he sent to Gibbon. The accompanying letter is now lost, but it caused Gibbon to lose his temper and he replied (January 1783) in the style of a newly arrived aristocrat putting an annoying social upstart in his proper place. The two men then exchanged epistolary insults for several weeks, and Gibbon continued the controversy one-sidedly in the notes to his History and in his Memoirs. In 1784 he embellished a footnote with a jest about Dr. Priestley's 'scanty creed'; two years later he solemnly indicated two rather harmless passages in Priestley's book and warned that 'at the first of these the priest, at the second the magistrate, may tremble!'; and in his Memoirs (written in 1791) he expressed a hope that Priestley's 'trumpet of sedition may at length awaken the magistrates of a free country'. As Gibbon ordinarily was kind-hearted and polite, such an outburst of bad manners, so long continued, can best be explained by the nervous strain under which he was labouring.[33]

For a year Gibbon stayed in London, continuing to attend meetings of Parliament and hoping to find a place whose salary was large enough to meet his needs but which would allow him leisure to complete his History. He thought of a post on the Board of Customs and Excise, or of a secretaryship in the embassy at Paris, or even of being named minister at Berne, but neither Shelburne nor Fox was willing to help him. At last, after several months of fidgeting and nervous waiting, he made up his mind to return to Switzerland. He announced his 'irrevocable decision' in July 1783, and on 15 September he left London for Lausanne.

In his early letters from Lausanne Gibbon frequently expressed his joy at being relieved from the heavy burden of a seat in Parliament, and he presently convinced himself that well-meaning friends had manœuvred him into a seat which he had never wanted. Soon after his arrival in Lausanne he arranged with Holroyd to get newspaper accounts of the debates in Parliament, but as time passed and he became settled in his Swiss environment, he lost even this slight enthusiasm for British politics. Before long he was writing to Holroyd: 'I never was a very warm Patriot and I grow every day a Citizen of the World. The scramble for power and profit at Westminster or St. James's and the names of Pitt and Fox become less interesting to me than those of Caesar and Pompey.' A few months later he declared that he was indifferent as to the outcome of 'the combat of Achilles Pitt and Hector Fox'.[34]

About three months after Gibbon's departure from England the

View of the lake and mountains from the terrace of Gibbon's house in Lausanne

young William Pitt became prime minister, at the age of twenty-four, and immediately launched an extensive programme of reform. On more than one occasion Gibbon praised Pitt in his letters, but 'the Revolution' or 'the Earthquake', as he not inappropriately called it, 'threw down all the men and systems of which I had any knowledge and the Country seems to be governed by a set of most respectable boys, who were in school half a dozen years ago'.[35] Before long, however, the much greater revolution in France took Gibbon completely by surprise.

In the spring of 1789 Gibbon was preoccupied with Deyverdun's lingering illness and death (on 4 July), and did not show grave concern over the disturbances in France. Moreover, as M. Necker seemed to be popular with the early leaders of the Revolution, Gibbon was sure that his friend would not let things go too far. In fact as 'Legislator of the French Monarchy' Necker might re-organize France as a constitutional monarchy on the British model. Before long, however, Gibbon learned that his hopes had been based on idle dreams, and that events were going to follow a very different course. He began using bitter language about the French, repeatedly referring to them as 'cannibals', making the word 'democrate' an abusive epithet, and even referring to the 'daemon of democracy' as the 'blackest daemon in hell'.[36]

Many factors contributed to Gibbon's disillusionment. When Necker fell from power (September 1790), he and his wife fled to Switzerland, where Gibbon saw them frequently and listened sympathetically to their harrowing accounts of what was happening in France. By this time Switzerland was crowded with fleeing French aristocrats, and while these *émigrés* made a bad impression upon Gibbon, he often believed their panicky tales. Gibbon seems to have been especially disturbed by the fate of the French king. When Louis XVI was executed (January 1793) Gibbon was tempted to wear mourning, and when he decided against it, he was roundly abused for his pusillanimity by Sheffield.[37] More substantial considerations may also have turned Gibbon against France, for soon after he settled in Lausanne, he had invested £1300 in French Government bonds which the Revolution rendered worthless.[38]

Gibbon's most serious complaint against the French, however, was that they were spreading their 'democratical ideas' throughout Europe, stirring up sedition, and waging war against peaceful peoples. Early in 1791 he wrote in his Memoirs:

> The fanatic missionaries of sedition have scattered the seeds of discontent in our [Swiss] cities and villages, which had flourished above two hundred and fifty years without fearing the approach of war, or feeling the weight of government. Many individuals, and some communities, appear to be infected with the French disease, the wild theories of equal and boundless freedom: but I trust that the body of the people will be faithful to their sovereign and themselves; and I am satisfied that the failure or success of a revolt would equally terminate in the ruin of the country. While the Aristocracy of Bern protects the happiness, it is superfluous to enquire whether it is founded in the rights of man. . . .[39]

Gibbon had wandered far since the day in 1763 when, assuming the character of a Swedish visitor, he sadly complained that the Vaudois would never rise in rebellion against the tyrants of Berne.

Gibbon was quick to accept the views set forth by Burke in his famous *Reflections on the French Revolution*. This tract was published early in November 1790, and within two weeks Gibbon wrote his publisher in London that he 'thirsted' for a copy. Reading the book raised him to ecstasy, and he wrote to Lord Sheffield: 'Burke's book is a most admirable medicine against the French disease, which has made too much progress even in this happy country. I admire his eloquence, I approve his politics, I adore his chivalry, and I can even forgive his superstition.' A few months later Gibbon wrote Sheffield that such moderate English reformers as Grey, Sheridan, and Erskine 'have talents for mischief', and urged him to 'remember the proud fabric of the French Monarchy. Not four years ago it stood founded, as it might seem, on the rock of time, force, and opinion, supported by the triple Aristocracy of the Church, the Nobility, and the Parliaments. They are crumbled into dust, they are vanished from the earth.'[40]

In Gibbon's opinion a major cause of France's collapse was to be found in the *philosophes* who attacked the fundamental ideas upon which the *ancien régime* had rested. He therefore began to question the merits of that liberty which he had once so fervently espoused. 'I have sometimes thought', he stated in 1791, 'of writing a dialogue of the dead, in which Lucian, Erasmus, and Voltaire should mutually acknowledge the danger of exposing an *old* superstition to the contempt of the blind and fanatic multitude.'[41] And in an amazing passage in his appendix to Gibbon's Memoirs, Lord Sheffield tells us that by 1791 Gibbon had become 'a warm and zealous advocate of every sort of old establishment, which he marked in various ways, sometimes rather ludicrously; and I recollect, in a circle where French affairs were the topic, and some Portuguese present, he, seemingly with seriousness, argued in favour of the Inquisition at Lisbon, and said that he would not, at the present moment, give up even that old establishment'.[42] In Gibbon's opinion, the damage had been done by the French *philosophes* whom he had always criticized, even in his early *Essai sur l'étude de la littérature*.

Gibbon thus completed his long and wide-ranging political odyssey. He had been in turn a Jacobite, a disciple of Locke and Montesquieu, a Tory, a Whig, a friend of Wilkes and Fox, a critic of North's policies in America but a defender of his use of armed force to maintain what he considered Britain's rights over her rebellious colonies, a placeman under North, and a cosmopolitan admirer of Swiss liberty. And he developed a hatred of the French Revolution and an admiration of Burke's intemperance. In the end his emotional reactions overbalanced his rational judgement.

One further aspect of Gibbon's political decline must be noted in passing. When Eliot refused further political support to Gibbon in

1780, each politely expressed a hope that their private friendship would continue, but the two men saw as little of each other as possible thereafter. Gibbon was deeply hurt, of course, and Eliot apparently was embarrassed by what he had done. When Gibbon published the second and third volumes of *The Decline and Fall* a few months later, he sent copies to his cousin, but Eliot failed even to return formal thanks. A few weeks later Gibbon learned that the Eliots had been in London for a month without letting him know. 'I instantly wrote a note to express my surprise and concern, — a dead silence of four days terminated only by a mute, blank, formal visit', he wrote to his stepmother, adding the comment, in parentheses, '(they are an odd family)'. When the North ministry fell, Gibbon wrote, 'The Eliots, whom I see *sometimes*, are well and as you may suppose, triumphant.' A few months later he reported that 'the Eliots are still in town, we meet seldom, but with the utmost propriety and equal regard'. Then came 'the Earthquake'. Pitt became prime minister on 19 December 1783, and within six weeks Eliot was created Baron Eliot of St. Germans. Nine months later Gibbon sent Eliot a pompous and visibly insincere letter of congratulation.[43] Eliot apparently did not reply, and the two men never met again.

Nevertheless Gibbon's encounters with the Eliots were not yet over. When the two men first discussed a seat in Parliament for Gibbon, they agreed to share the election costs (£2400) equally, but, as Gibbon did not have the ready money, the wealthy Eliot undertook to bear the whole cost of the election while Gibbon promised to pay his half to Eliot's second son (John Eliot) after eight years, when the boy came of age. When reporting this arrangement to Holroyd, Gibbon expressed the hope that he would then have the money, either from his book or by inheritance from his Aunt Hester. He added, however, that if he still was unable to pay, he would leave the Buriton estate to John in his Will.[44] We hear nothing more of Gibbon's debt until 1780, when Eliot refused to renominate him. Gibbon then expressed regret that he could not pay and craved a little indulgence.* This letter was followed by silence for eight years, until Gibbon returned to London to see his last three volumes through the press. Shortly before his return to Lausanne he signed a Will (14 July 1788) by which he left the greater part of his estate to Eliot's two younger sons, John and William. (The eldest son, Edward, presumably would inherit the bulk of his father's property.) Four days later Gibbon wrote his last letter to Eliot, formally expressing his sorrow at not having seen him during his year in England, promising to write to Lady Eliot from Lausanne, inviting his sons, 'particularly the youngest and least busy, to visit me in my retirement', but saying nothing of the debt or the Will.[45]

The last act of the comedy came three years later. Gibbon's maternal uncle, Sir Stanier Porten, died in June 1789, leaving a widow and two children, Stanier and Charlotte. Heretofore Gibbon had paid little attention to these cousins, but in his Will of 1788 he left each of the children £2000. When Deyverdun died a few weeks later, Gibbon was left in sole possession of the house at Lausanne. In his loneliness Gibbon thought of adopting Charlotte and taking her to Switzerland to care for him in his old age. 'She might either remain a spinster (the case is not without example)', he wrote to Sheffield, 'or marry some Swiss of my choice, who would encrease and enliven our society: and both would have the strongest motives for kind and dutiful behaviour.'[46] We are not surprised to learn that Charlotte's mother refused to agree to this odd arrangement. Gibbon retained his regard for the family, however, and made other plans for their welfare. Early in 1791 he directed Lord Sheffield to destroy his Will of 1788, saying that he had prepared another 'on more rational principles'. This new Will was signed at Lausanne on 1 October 1791, and by it Gibbon left the greater part of his estate to Sir Stanier's two children, whom he characterized as 'the nearest,

* Gibbon was not quite candid when he said that he could not pay the £1200 he owed Eliot. Six weeks before he made this statement he had sold the copyright on the first three volumes of *The Decline and Fall* to his publisher for £4000. (Norton, *Bibliography* 45.)

the most indigent, and the most deserving of my relations'. He then explained the change of heirs by saying that Lord Eliot's sons did not need the money while Sir Stanier's did.[47] This statement was correct on both counts, but it would have been equally correct in 1788. Why, then, did Gibbon change his Will at this late date? Perhaps it was because he regarded this act as providing an appropriate farewell to Lord Eliot and to his own 'cursed political life'.

CHAPTER SIX

THE HUMANIST TURNS TO HISTORY

DURING his omnivorous childhood Gibbon gulped down parts of several histories, a few of which were good, but most of which were not. Chief among the latter was the *Universal History*, a work in twenty volumes compiled by a group of hacks and published between 1740 and 1749. In 1751, when Gibbon was only fourteen years old, he took delight in going through its volumes dealing with the ancient world. They taught him something of the general course of human events, as this was commonly understood in the eighteenth century, but they did not inspire him with a desire to write history or show him how it should be written. Oxford, too, failed to arouse in him an ambition to become a historian, and even M. Pavillard, though an honorary professor of Latin and Ancient History at the Académie de Lausanne, apparently did little to encourage his pupil to study history.

Pavillard's educational programme closely followed that devised by the humanists of the sixteenth century to train classical scholars. Its hard core consisted of an intensive study of the Latin and Greek languages and literature, supplemented by sketchy introductions to a few other matters which might contribute to a better understanding of the ancient classics. Though Gibbon continued to read widely for pleasure, and though a few histories found a place among the books he read, his serious studies followed this classical curriculum.

While at Lausanne Gibbon carefully read the Latin writers, together with the commentaries of modern classical scholars; he wrote brief essays in French on topics that occurred to him in the course of these studies; and he carried on a Latin correspondence with professors in Paris, Göttingen, and Zürich. In his letters he discussed various difficulties he had found in the texts he studied and, following the practice of the classical scholars of his day, he suggested various rather arbitrary emendations of these texts. A few of his suggestions were good, but some were not — as his correspondents tactfully told him. The essays, on the other hand, dealt with literary criticism or with various aspects of Roman life. During his last months at Lausanne, for example, he undertook a critical study of Sir Isaac Newton's chronology of the ancient world, and soon after his return to England he prepared a hundred-page treatise on ancient weights and measures. The most important product of this humanistic phase of Gibbon's intellectual development, however, was his *Essai sur l'étude de la littérature*.[1]

This little book was written over a period of about three years. Every paragraph was revised time and time again, but Gibbon's Journal enables us to disentangle the resultant jumble and to fix the approximate date when each was written. Gibbon first planned the essay at Lausanne, where he wrote several pages in March and April 1758, and a few months later he completed a first draft at Buriton. He then requested a certain Dr. Maty to read and criticize the manuscript. Maty complied, and as a result of his criticisms Gibbon suppressed a third, added a third, and altered a third of what he had written. He then put the manuscript away in a drawer, where it lay undisturbed for more than two years. In April 1761 Gibbon returned to his task, adding a long section, and in the following July he published the essay as a small duodecimo volume of 159 pages.

The composition of the *Essai* thus fell into four distinct periods, each separated from its predecessor by important events in the author's intellectual life: his return from studious Lausanne to rural England; the criticisms of Dr. Maty and (what was in the long run vastly more important) Gibbon's discovery and reading of the histories of Robertson and Hume; and finally his 'tryal of the evidence of Christianity'. In the parts of the *Essai* that he wrote during the first period Gibbon concerned himself primarily with defending classical studies against the attacks of d'Alembert and other French *philosophes*, whom he accused of valuing only mathematics and natural science. In replying to their attacks upon the study of ancient literature Gibbon argued that the study of the classics improves the taste and trains the intellect, and he called to witness a number of great men who in youth had distinguished themselves by such studies. This much he wrote at Lausanne. In the second section, written at Buriton, he discussed the problems and methods of humanistic literary criticism; in the third he dealt critically with a few problems in early Roman history; and in a long concluding section he gave an account of Rome's pagan religion.

Throughout the *Essai* Gibbon wrote as a humanist defending the study of classical literature, but there are passages that show that he was beginning to think along historical lines. 'The history of empires', he declared in the opening sentence of his book, 'is the story of man's misery. The history of learning is that of his greatness and happiness. If a thousand considerations should render studies of the latter sort dear to a philosopher, this reflection ought to make them dear to all who love humanity.' A little later he declared that it would be a worth-while task for a skilful man to 'trace the revolutions in religions, governments, and manners, which have successively misled, afflicted, and corrupted mankind'.[2] But he gave no hint that he was considering writing history himself.

The section of the *Essai* that deals with Virgil's *Georgics*[3] is of especial interest. After reminding his readers of the frightful damage that Italy suffered when Sulla's discharged veterans ran amuck (about 80 B.C.), Gibbon praised Augustus's handling of the veteran problem fifty years later. When Augustus disbanded his army, he allotted a small farm to each of his veterans and, when they demanded cash bonuses that he could not pay, he commissioned Virgil to write the *Georgics*. This poem is said by Gibbon to have depicted the pleasures of country life so charmingly that the veterans patiently

H

waited thirty years for their bonuses! 'In my opinion', Gibbon stated in his concluding paragraph, 'Vergil was not simply a writer describing rural labours. He was a new Orpheus sounding his lyre in order to calm the ferocity of savages and to unite them by the bonds of custom and law. His poem worked this miracle.'

If we wish to understand this fantastic interpretation of the *Georgics* we must remember that at about the time Gibbon conceived it his father was strongly urging him to buy a seat in Parliament and that he was flattering himself with the patriotic thought that in Parliament he 'might be one day the instrument of some good to my country'. But he preferred to continue his scholarly career: if Virgil could render such valuable aid to Augustus and to Rome, surely a scholar might accomplish something equally worth while for England by studying literature rather than sitting in Parliament.

Despite frequent distractions Gibbon continued his classical studies while he was serving in the militia. He resumed the study of Greek and went through the entire *Iliad*, a large part of the *Odyssey*, and Longinus's essay *On the Sublime*; he read widely and deeply in the *Mèmoires* of the French Academy of Inscriptions (he had recently purchased the first twenty volumes of that great collection for £20: 'nor would it have been easy', he wrote many years later, 'by any other expenditure of the same sum, to have procured so large and lasting a fund of rational enjoyment'[4]); and he developed an interest in Erasmus, whom he praised for having brought light to Europe after a thousand years of intellectual darkness and whom he continued to admire throughout his life. At this time Gibbon was a classicist centring his studies around ancient Latin literature, and so great was the influence of these studies upon his subsequent intellectual development that a recent critic has hailed him as 'the last of the humanists'.[5]

Many of the Italian humanists had written histories, but, since history as such had no place in M. Pavillard's educational programme, Gibbon did not become acquainted with them. Nevertheless he found time to read a few historical works during his last three years in Lausanne. One was the Abbé Vertot's *Histoire des révolutions de la république romaine* (1719), of which he later wrote that 'his works read like novels, which they resemble much too closely'. He renewed his interest in Conyers Middleton, whose *Free Enquiry* had once shocked him into the Roman Church, and studied that author's *Life of Cicero.* He also 'observed with a critical eye the progress and abuse of Sacerdotal power' in Giannone's *Civil History of Naples* (1742). His greatest delight, however, came from the 'frequent perusal of Montesquieu'. Properly speaking, Montesquieu was a political theorist, or perhaps a sociologist, rather than a historian, but he often invoked history to illustrate his ideas, and his *Considérations sur les causes de la grandeur des romains et de leur décadence* (1734) opened up new approaches to the study of Roman history.

Shortly after his return to England in 1758 Gibbon read the recently published histories of Robertson and Hume. At the same time, however, he was also reading the erudite studies of French classical scholars in the *Mémoires* of the Academy of Inscriptions. He was impressed by their learning and careful scholarship and, when he found that Hume did not measure up to their standards in such matters, his first thought was to dismiss the historian as 'ingenious but superficial'. Presently, however, he came to think more highly of the historian; he spoke feelingly of his 'original philosophic genius'; and at length he decided that he wanted to write books like Hume's on historical subjects.[6]

Even before the publication of his *Essai* (July 1761) Gibbon had begun considering topics for a historical essay. In April of that year he thought of writing a book about the expedition of Charles VIII of France into Italy, and he stated in his Journal that he had already written a brief study of Charles's right to the throne of Naples. He soon gave up the project, however, and Charles VIII was laid aside and forgotten. In August of this same year Gibbon again mentioned his search for a suitable historical subject, and listed several topics that he had been considering. Some were of a romantic nature — 'The Crusade of Richard Cœur de Lion', 'Philip Sidney', and, most important of all, 'Sir Walter Raleigh'. Others were political, perhaps showing Whiggish overtones — 'The Barons against John and Henry III', and 'The History of the Liberty of the Swiss'. Another gave evidence of Gibbon's abiding interest in humanism — 'Florence in the Days of the Medicis'.[7] It is curious that all but two of these topics deal with phases of English history, and therefore owe little or nothing to Gibbon's experiences at Lausanne, and that it apparently had not occurred to him that he might exploit his knowledge of the classics by writing about Roman history.

A year later Gibbon recorded in his Journal that although he had begun the biography of Raleigh he had abandoned the project because he was unable to think of anything that had not already been said about that hero. He also discarded all the other topics except the two which dealt with foreign countries: the history of Swiss liberty and Florence under the Medicis. After ruling out the history of Switzerland because he knew no German, he decided upon the history of Florence. 'What makes this subject still more precious', he noted in his Journal, 'are two fine *morceaux* for a Philosophical historian, and which are essential parts of it, the Restoration of Learning in Europe by Lorenzo de Medicis and the character and fate of Savonarola. The Medicis employed letters to strengthen their power and their enemies opposed them with religion.'[8] (The Medicis apparently used literary men in much the way Gibbon had conjectured that Augustus used Virgil). Nothing came of all this day-dreaming, however, for the war with France was almost over, and Gibbon was planning his second trip to Lausanne.

Even while Gibbon was thus toying with the idea of writing history, he did not discontinue his classical studies. During his last year in the militia he found time to read his favourite Latin poets again and again, to write a long and laudatory criticism of Bishop

Hurd's edition of Horace's *Epistles*, and to continue his Greek studies. While at Paris in the spring of 1763 he visited the city's famous libraries and met a few scholars, but he did little serious reading and no writing. A week after his arrival in Lausanne, however, he told his father: 'I have got a few books together and am busy upon the ancient Geography of Italy and the reviewing my Roman history and antiquities.' Two months later he wrote to his stepmother about 'a considerable work I am engaged in . . . a Description of the ancient Geography of Italy, taken from the Original writers'.[9]

At first Gibbon's plans for this considerable work were rather vague, but he began his researches by reading the ancient geographers and hunting out passages of geographic interest in the poets. He soon discovered, however, that this arduous task had long since been adequately performed by classical scholars. He therefore procured the ponderous folios of two seventeenth-century *érudits* — Clüver's *Italia Antiqua* (1624) and Nardini's *Roma Vetus* (1666) — and during the next three months he ploughed through almost two thousand large pages of Latin, taking notes as he went along, recording in his Journal day by day which pages he had read and summarizing their contents. On several occasions he wrote brief essays on points that had interested him in that day's reading. But this heavy schedule left him neither time nor energy for writing his own projected book on Italy.

At last, on 3 December 1763, Gibbon remarked in his Journal that he had that day finished reading Clüver's *Italia Antiqua*. 'Tâche vraiment laborieuse!' he exclaimed, after which he proceeded with a judicious criticism of its author. He recognized Clüver's vast learning and his careful thoroughness, but found fault with his diffuseness and with the bad arrangement of his materials. A more important criticism accused Clüver of putting undue trust in the ancient writers, for his efforts to harmonize the contradictory statements of ancient authors often led him to make drastic changes in their texts. 'Cluvier sweats blood and water to reconcile these texts', Gibbon commented on one occasion.[10] Clüver thus disillusioned Gibbon regarding the merits of classical scholarship and unintentionally convinced him that the ancient writers were not so infallible as the classicists of that day fondly believed.

When Gibbon first considered writing a book on the geography of Italy he was still a belated classicist at heart, and he planned a book that would be of interest and use to students of literature with scholarly tastes like his own — *érudits* of the sort he had championed in his *Essai sur l'étude de la littérature*. 'A student of Literature', he remarked in his Journal on the day he began reading Clüver, 'would like to know even the tiniest corners of these celebrated countries, where the smallest village is famous in history or poetry.' His early plans were for a book to meet such needs. He would describe Italy province by province, list the towns of each, tell something of their importance, and quote what the ancient poets had said about them. When Gibbon discovered that this was just what Clüver had done, he revised his plans, and in his Journal he told how a philosopher would improve upon the work of the classicists. He would include a discussion of the natural products of each province, the migrations of its peoples, their laws and their characters. He would then show how the configuration of the country, its climate, and its location influenced the customs of its people and what befell them. And he would arrange his narrative differently. Clüver began at the north-west corner of Italy and zigzagged his way south to Bruttium; Gibbon decided to start from Rome and proceed in the order of Roman conquests. 'The reader', he explained, 'would then easily follow the progress of Roman arms and Livy's narrative.'[11] The young classicist was becoming interested in history, but he was still primarily a classicist none the less.

Gibbon became quite enthusiastic about the book he now envisaged, which he planned to call *Recueil géographique sur l'Italie*, and even persuaded himself that it would appeal to a wide audience. 'It could make a profit for a publisher,' he remarked in his Journal, 'reach a tenth Edition, and become a Classic for Colleges, travellers, and even for men of letters.' But the labour of reading Clüver had exhausted him; he was bored by this learned but pedantic scholar; and during his last months at Lausanne he devoted himself largely to general reading and to social life. Not until the middle of February did he resume serious study, and even then he was often distracted by his difficulties with Suzanne Curchod and his brisk flirtation with 'la petite femme', Madame Seigneux. Gibbon gathered a little additional material for the book while in Italy; he translated part of it into English while at Genoa; and he wrote to his stepmother from Florence that he had not lost sight of the undertaking. He then added, 'I do not despair of being able one day to produce something by way of a Description of ancient Italy which may be of some use to the publick and of some credit to myself.' We hear nothing more about the *Recueil.* Gibbon remarked briefly in his Memoirs, 'I filled a folio common-place book with my collections and remarks on the geography of Italy', apparently referring to what Lord Sheffield edited and published in the second edition (but not in the first) of the *Miscellaneous Works* (1814) under the title 'Nomina Gentesque Antiquae Italiae'.[12] The manuscript of the *Recueil* has been lost.

Meantime Gibbon had been rounding out his knowledge of ancient Italy with the aid of materials which are now considered basic by historians of antiquity, but which were largely unknown to the classical scholars of Gibbon's day. During his last weeks in Lausanne he happened to read a little book about ancient medals by the English essayist, Joseph Addison, and he became so interested in the subject that he hunted up and read Spanheim's scholarly two-volume work on ancient coins. This book laid the foundations of the modern science of numismatics. While travelling in Italy Gibbon was fascinated by the collections of coins in the museums, and he spent many hours studying them. It was at this time, too, that Gibbon learned the value of ancient inscriptions. He copied a few into a notebook during his travels in Italy, and in his Journal he commented upon 'the very useful light [the inscriptions] throw on the history, Geography, and Economy of their time'. Two weeks later he declared that 'by means of [these inscriptions] we can often explain, confirm, and correct even the historians'.[13]

Gibbon also began showing an interest in archaeology. While in Paris he had seen Montfaucon's *L'Antiquité expliquée* (1719) — an enormous work in fifteen folio volumes which laid the foundations for the modern study of Italian archaeology — but he had neither the time nor the inclination to study it just then. In Lausanne, however, he found time to read long passages from it. In his criticism of Clüver he remarked that 'fortunately a scholar can now embellish his work with the results of two new types of erudition, the Etruscan monuments and those of Herculaneum'. Early in the next year he read and took notes on a thirty-page article dealing with the discoveries at Herculaneum.[14]

Then came Gibbon's epoch-marking visit to Rome. Here the romantic side of his nature gained the upper hand for a time, and he went about 'almost in a dream'. This enthusiasm reached its climax a few evenings later when, as he sat musing amid the ruins of the Capitol, the idea of writing a history of Rome first started to his mind.[15] We do not know exactly what sort of book he envisaged on that famous evening, but it is safe to say that it bore little resemblance to *The Decline and Fall* which came several years later. In fact he tells us explicitly that his original plan was limited to describing the decay of the city rather than that of the Empire. He had been studying Nardini, whose book devoted careful attention to the erection of Rome's monuments, and Gibbon apparently planned to complete the story by telling of their destruction.

Gibbon returned to England in June 1765 after an absence of two and a half years. He settled at Buriton, where he led the life of a country squire and where, in spite of occasional visits to London, he was thoroughly lonesome and unhappy. He did not abandon his scholarly ambitions, but he was at a loss for something to do.

The Roman Forum in Gibbon's day

Again he turned to the romantic East, and presently he composed, in French, a hundred-page 'Mémoire sur la monarchie des mèdes', drawing much of his material from d'Herbelot's *Bibliothèque orientale*, with which he had become acquainted in his Oxford days. Here, as in his earliest writings, Gibbon was especially interested in problems of chronology, but he also suggested various reasons for the decline and fall of the Median Empire, some of which reappear in *The Decline and Fall* as causes of the fall of Rome. In his later years Gibbon was not proud of this essay (he made no mention of it in his letters or his Memoirs), but it is important for us as his first attempt to write formal history.

Meantime Gibbon's loneliness had been alleviated by the arrival in England of his Swiss friend, Georges Deyverdun. During the winter Deyverdun worked as a clerk in London, but he passed four summers as Gibbon's guest at Buriton. The two friends conversed at length on literary topics, and their discussions revived Gibbon's idea of writing a history of Switzerland in French. Deyverdun promised his aid in translating German sources, but the work progressed slowly and not until the summer of 1767 did Gibbon actually begin to write. When he had completed two chapters, he had them read before a group of literary men in London whose frank criticisms persuaded him to drop the project. One man, however, was favourably impressed by Gibbon's manuscript. This was David Hume, whom Gibbon had admired for several years and whom he had recently met. Gibbon showed him the manuscript, and a few weeks later the philosopher wrote a kind letter praising the book but criticizing the author for writing in French. Gibbon was greatly elated by this letter, as well he might be, and he took Hume's suggestions to heart. Thereafter he wrote in English.

Little attention need be paid to Gibbon's other writings of this period. He and Deyverdun planned a periodical whose lengthy book reviews and brief articles on literary matters would inform European readers regarding recent English publications. The first volume of the *Mémoires littéraires de la Grande-Bretagne* appeared in April

1768, but the publisher sold so few copies that he would not undertake a second volume. Another publisher was found, however, and the second volume appeared early in 1769. It fared no better than the first. Thoroughly discouraged, Deyverdun returned to Europe as the paid companion of a young British aristocrat making the Grand Tour, and the *Mémoires littéraires* were forgotten.

The failure of the history of Switzerland and of the *Mémoires*, capped by Deyverdun's departure, heightened Gibbon's loneliness and feeling of frustration, and presently drove him to an act of which he had little reason to be proud. Early in 1770, when his prospects seemed bleak indeed, he published a bitter and anonymous pamphlet entitled *Critical Observations on the Sixth Book of the Aeneid*, in which he viciously attacked a widely respected scholar, William Warburton, Bishop of Gloucester. The bishop had published a large work of Christian apologetics entitled *The Divine Legation of Moses* (2 vols., 1737–41), in which he maintained, among other things, that Virgil's account of Aeneas's descent into the lower world (in the sixth book of the *Aeneid*) was based on the ritual of the Eleusinian mysteries. Gibbon had read this part of *The Divine Legation* while in the militia and had been annoyed by what he regarded as a denigration of his favourite poet. In his Journal he reported having 'perused the VIth Book of Virgil and the System of Warburton upon it', and declared that he had 'found many things to say, to explain the one and destroy the other'. Two years later he again mentioned Warburton unfavourably, and after six more years he published his criticisms. He did not do himself justice, and his pamphlet attracted little attention. In later years Gibbon was rather ashamed of this performance, and in his Memoirs he wrote, 'I cannot forgive myself the contemptuous treatment of a man who, with all his faults, was entitled to my esteem; and I can less forgive, in a personal attack, the cowardly concealment of my name and character.'[16]

Two years later Gibbon seemed to be picking a quarrel with another clergyman, Richard Hurd, Archdeacon of Gloucester and a protégé of Warburton. While in the militia he had studied Hurd's commentary on Horace's *Epistles* and had praised it highly in a forty-page essay. Among other things he declared that this was the work of 'one of those valuable authors who cannot be read without improvement'. But when Hurd published a book on *The Prophecies concerning the Christian Church* (1772), Gibbon sent him a long and disputatious letter, criticizing his use of the prophecies of Daniel. Gibbon did not sign his name to the letter, but gave an address to which a reply might be sent. Hurd answered with a careful and courteous letter, and Gibbon started a reply, but after writing one page he dropped the matter. Not until after Gibbon's death, more than twenty years later, did Hurd learn who his correspondent had been.[17]

Gibbon's darkest days were now nearly over, for in November 1770, only a few months after the publication of the *Critical Observations*, his father died. Gibbon was thus relieved of a heavy burden. At last he could leave Buriton and establish himself permanently in London (1772). More than seven years had gone by since his return to England from Italy, and in his Memoirs he pictures these dreary and frustrating years as wholly lost. This pessimistic judgement is not just. It was during these years that he finally decided what he wished to do with the remainder of his life. He made up his mind that he would rather be a historian than a humanist or classicist, that he would centre his studies around history rather than literature, that he would deal with the later years of the Roman Empire rather than a more modern period, and that he would write in English rather than French. Moreover, he had read the principal ancient and modern writers on his chosen field and had thus laid the foundations for the History he now set himself to write.

Gibbon was not the first historian to speculate and write upon the decline and fall of a great empire. In fact the story of the rise and fall of empires has always been a favourite theme with historians. Towards the end of the third millennium before Christ a historian living at Ur of the Chaldees drew up a list of the various kings by whom, he believed, Sumeria had been ruled since antediluvian times. He arranged these kings in groups, called dynasties, and for him history was largely the story of the rise and fall of these successive dynasties. Primitive theologians then undertook to explain the story. These men had long been in the habit of considering disasters of any sort as divinely sent punishments for sin, and now they attributed the rise and fall of dynasties to the will of the gods. They declared that the founder of a dynasty had been successful because his goodness and piety had won him the favour of the gods, but that the dynasty fell when the sins of his successors caused them to lose divine favour. This theological and moral explanation of the rise and fall of empires dominated the historical thinking of the Near East for many centuries, colouring even the historical books of the Old Testament.

The classic Greek historians approached their subject in a very different spirit, seeking to explain the course of history by purely natural causes. Thucydides, writing about 400 B.C., refused to invoke divine wrath as the cause of Athens's recent defeat at the hands of the Spartans, and shortly after 150 B.C. Polybius ascribed Rome's rapid conquest of the Mediterranean world to her social and military organization and to the sterling but secular virtues of her people.

The outstanding Roman historians of the late republican period believed that the political troubles that overwhelmed Rome in the first century B.C. came as a consequence of the unparalleled immorality of the day. Sallust, writing about 40 B.C., declared that the great moral decline began soon after the destruction of Carthage (146 B.C.), when the Romans no longer feared their ancient enemy and therefore gave free rein to luxury and debauchery. A few years later Livy announced that he was going to write a history of Rome in order to remind his fellow citizens of the virtues of their ancestors, hoping thus to check the moral decline which he saw dragging

Rome to ruin. These writers did not picture Rome's troubles as a divinely sent punishment for sin, however, but as the natural result of the debilitation brought by luxury and vice.

In the centuries following the Golden Age of Augustus, writers often lamented the decline of Rome in their day. Sometimes they attributed this decline to the loss of liberty, sometimes they spoke of her ageing or senescence, and sometimes they invoked moral causes. But though alarmed by what they saw about them, they could not bring themselves to prophesy the fall of their city or the collapse of her empire. Even after the plagues of the second century, the wars and economic disasters of the third, and the barbarian invasions of the fourth and fifth centuries, men continued to speak proudly of *Roma aeterna* — 'Eternal Rome'. In the year A.D. 400 Claudian — 'the last Roman poet' — declared that 'there will never be a limit to the empire of Rome'. Things might be going badly at the moment, but Rome's ancient power and glory would return. She had not 'fallen', and she would never fall.

Sometimes, however, the peoples whom Rome had conquered felt differently about it. Leaders knew that, for the time being, armed rebellion against Rome would be hopeless, but they kept discontent alive by circulating anti-Roman propaganda among their restless fellow subjects. This propaganda often took the form of prophecies foretelling a dire fate for Rome, and one of these prophecies requires attention because of its great influence upon later historians. This is the famous prophecy of the Four Monarchies.[18]

The author of this prophecy supposedly had lived in the remote past and had predicted that four great empires, each more terrible than its predecessor, were destined to rule the world. After the fall of the Fourth Monarchy, however, divine aid would usher in a Fifth Monarchy which would be universal and eternal. Under its benign rule all men would be supremely happy. The prophet actually lived in Syria about 200 B.C., and though he used obscure language, of course, it is clear that his prophecy was directed against Antiochus III, the Macedonian king then ruling that country.

The four monarchies were easily identifiable as Assyria, Media, Persia, and Macedonia, and vague allusions convinced those who read the prophecy aright that in their day the terrible Fourth Monarchy had almost run its course. True believers expected its speedy downfall and eagerly awaited the coming of the glorious Fifth Monarchy, under which the happy world would again be ruled by Oriental kings, priests, and gods.

Shortly after Scipio defeated Antiochus at Magnesia (189 B.C.), a Roman chronicler named Aemilius Sura learned of this prophecy (which by this time was known throughout the Near East) and straightway claimed for Rome the honour of being the Fifth Monarchy. A quarter of a century later the prophecy appeared in the biblical Book of Daniel, where the independent Jewish state, for which Judas Maccabaeus was then fighting, was indicated as the Fifth Monarchy. During the next several centuries the prophecy was kept alive by writers who sometimes pictured Rome as the Fifth Monarchy, while others, counting Media and Persia as one, made her the Fourth Monarchy, fated soon to perish. Interpretations of this prophecy might differ, but for many centuries historians continued to divide the past into four periods and to predict, implicitly or explicitly, that their present governments would soon fall and that all mankind would then live happily under the glorious, long-awaited, and eternal Fifth Monarchy.

Even in Livy's day there were many people to whom his history, telling how the inhabitants of a village on the Tiber went out and subjugated the world, seemed absurdly parochial, and who knew that many things had happened that were not recorded in any of his 142 volumes. Several writers then published world histories to include what patriotic Roman writers had left out. The most important of these opposition historians was a Gaul named Pompeius Trogus, who wrote about 30 B.C. In forty-four volumes he traced the rise and fall of empires from the time of Ninus, the mythical founder of Assyria, to the defeat of Antony and Cleopatra at Actium in 31 B.C. He was critical of Rome and the empires that had preceded her, and he so arranged his history that Rome appeared as the fourth world monarchy. In his own day Trogus was not highly regarded at Rome, probably because of his defective Roman patriotism, but two or three centuries later, when many people were glad to see Rome's orthodox history exploded, his book became more popular and a man named Justin made a rather full abridgement of it. Trogus's history did not survive the havoc of the early Middle Ages, but Justin's epitome was a widely used school-book throughout medieval and early modern times, and before 1850 it had appeared in more than 250 printed editions. Gibbon studied it carefully during his first stay in Lausanne, and discussed it learnedly with an eminent scholar in Zürich.

The most significant, and eventually the most effective, critics of the Roman Empire were the Christians. Even in New Testament times the author of Revelations had attacked Rome bitterly, calling her 'Babylon the Great' and predicting that her fall was imminent. This hostility continued for more than two centuries, until the patronage of Constantine (311) gave the Christians a strong position in the Empire. The Church then began to absorb the Empire, both politically and culturally, and Christian scholars undertook the task of showing how all history, pagan as well as Hebrew, had led up to the establishment and final victory of Christianity. They gave an important place in this story to Rome, whose history, they now discovered, was not all bad. The principal Christian scholar of this period was Jerome, whose *Chronicle* (published about 380) became the medieval historian's main guide to early times. In this work Jerome made Hebrew history, as recorded in the Old Testament, the backbone of world history down to the time of Christ, after which he was concerned primarily with the progress of Christianity. Around this central theme, however, he arranged the more noteworthy events in Near Eastern, Greek, and Roman history, relying upon pagan writers for his information. He was much indebted to Trogus, from whom (or from Justin) he took the theory of the Four Monarchies. Like Trogus, he identified Rome with the Fourth

Monarchy. Concerning the Fifth Monarchy he and his followers were vague, but many identified it with the Christian Church.

Jerome and his continuators thus designed a new pattern of world history that was accepted by most historians for the next several centuries. This magnificent story, which has been called the 'Christian Epic', traced the course of human events from Adam to the historian's own day; it covered the whole world (or at least the whole Christian world, which was all that mattered); and it had much to say of the rise and fall of ancient cities, states, and empires. But as all these tragedies and misfortunes were merely parts of God's great plan for the salvation of mankind, there was no need for a detailed inquiry into the immediate causes of individual events.

Medieval chroniclers who described the woes of Italy in the fifth century admitted that Rome had been humbled by the barbarians, but they did not say that she had fallen or indicate that a new era in world history had begun with Alaric's sack of Rome in 410, or with the expulsion of the last Roman emperor of the West (Romulus, nicknamed Augustulus) by Odoacer and his Goths in 476, or with any other comparable event. Moreover, just as the Holy Roman Emperors of the Middle Ages regarded themselves as the lawful successors of Augustus and Augustulus, invoking the doctrine of the 'translatio imperii ad Teutonicos' to justify their claims, so the historians of their day were sure that Rome, having survived her misfortunes, would continue to rule until the end of the world. Only a few visionaries, usually saints or heretics, continued to expect the immediate fall of Rome or implied that she had fallen at some time in the past. The 'fall of Rome' was a matter for theologians and the writers of apocalypses, not one for bona fide historians.

The first historians to put the fall of Rome in the past, and to assign it an important place in world history were humanists in the days of the Italian Renaissance. The medieval compilers of chronicles had usually been monks, writing from an ecclesiastical point of view, but their humanist successors were laymen, setting forth views current in the independent communes of northern Italy in the fourteenth and fifteenth centuries. They preferred city or national histories to world histories, and as they put no faith in prophecies, they jettisoned the Four Monarchies, along with other fundamental features of the Christian Epic. These humanists were enraptured by Cicero and his contemporaries, and they found Livy and Sallust more congenial writers than Jerome and Augustine. Their efforts to explain how the heroes of ancient Rome came to be superseded by priests and monks led them to formulate a new version of history, and to devise a new conception of the fall of Rome.

When classic and medieval historians spoke of the 'fall' of a city they usually envisaged its material destruction after a military defeat, as had been the case with Troy and Carthage or Nineveh and Persepolis, and in this sense Rome had not fallen. The humanists, on the other hand, conceived of Rome's 'fall' as primarily political and cultural — a falling off of literature, scholarship, and the arts. They declared Rome had 'fallen' in the fifth century and that her 'fall' had ushered in a thousand years of intellectual darkness, which was dissipated only by the rise of humanism in the fourteenth century.[19]

Petrarch (1304–74), 'the first modern scholar', was among the first to set forth the new humanistic view of the decline and fall of the Roman Empire. In his essays he distinguished sharply between ancient and modern times. The former he called *antiqua*, the latter *nova*, and he drew the dividing line at the conversion of Constantine. He admired the old pagan times, but he had only contempt for the cultural darkness of the Christian ages that followed. Petrarch's humanist successors usually accepted his division of history into two periods — ancient and modern — though they often criticized his denigration of early modern times, for they regarded these dark centuries as the seed-bed from which their own world sprang. This theory was ably launched by Biondo, whose *History from the Decline of the Roman Empire* (published 1439–53) devoted the first two of its three 'Decades' to the thousand years between 410 and 1442, while the third covered the next thirty years. Seventy-five years later Machiavelli gave classic expression to this view of history in the early chapters of his *Florentine Histories* (1525) — parts of which Gibbon had read before he went to Oxford, and re-read when studying Italian in London in 1759.

When the early humanists rejected the medieval conception of Rome's misfortunes as due, purely and simply, to the will of God, they found it necessary to provide new and more mundane explanations of that tragic event. But their efforts led to no very profound theories. As these humanists were patriots, proud of the independence and freedom of their communes, they found it easy to follow Tacitus and other ancient writers in attributing the decline of Rome to the loss of liberty in imperial times. Moreover, the political freedom of their communes was constantly threatened by the intrigues of the popes and emperors, which encouraged historians to attribute Rome's troubles in the fifth century to the unsettling activities of the Church and the Germanic invasions. Writers such as Machiavelli therefore prepared the way for Gibbon's famous phrase about 'the triumph of barbarism and religion'.

During the century of the Reformation, Protestant controversialists learned to bend this new view of history to their uses. They agreed with the humanists that literature and true learning had flourished in the great days of Rome, but had declined during the Dark Ages until they were restored by the humanists of the Renaissance. In the same way, they argued, pure Christianity had existed in New Testament times, but had been corrupted by the Church and had declined for many centuries until the Reformers restored true religion. Catholic writers, on the other hand, retained the older view of history, insisting that, just as Rome had never fallen, so the Christian Church had not declined or fallen, and it never would; and just as the Holy Roman Emperors were truly the successors of Augustus, so the popes were the true successors of Peter. Champions of each faction ransacked history in search of facts that would support their cause or injure that of their opponents, and they subjected the history put forward by their adversaries to the most exacting criticism. Eventually, however, the fires of controversy died down, and in the seventeenth century these theological polemicists gave way to *érudits* who devoted their lives to gathering and criticizing historical texts and documents. They collected enormous heaps of information about the past; they edited texts and wrote tremendously learned monographs on minute topics, filling huge folio volumes with their barbarous Latin; and they developed new and sharper methods of historical criticism. But ordinarily their interpretations of the past were neither profound nor exciting, and their books could be read only by the most patient scholars — by men such as Gibbon.

There was still one major problem which historians had to solve. When did the ancient world come to its end and when did the modern world begin? Many of the early humanists thought that the ancient world came to an end with Constantine, early in the fourth century, or else with Romulus Augustulus, late in the fifth, and they believed that modern times began immediately thereafter. This arrangement of history became unacceptable to scholars in the seventeenth century, for what they considered modern times had begun in the fifteenth century with the fall of Constantinople, the rise of humanism, or the discovery of America. A thousand years were thus left unaccounted for. Were these centuries ancient or modern? A few scholars tried to solve this difficulty by dating modern times from the coronation of Charlemagne in 800. This suggestion was accepted by such popularizers as Bossuet (1685) and Voltaire (1756), and we shall see that even Gibbon toyed with the idea for a moment, but it did not satisfy scholars for long. At last, in 1688, a German schoolmaster named Cellarius published a textbook in which he cut the Gordian knot by calling the years from Constantine to 1453 the 'Middle Ages'. This practice of dividing European history into three distinct periods — ancient, medieval, and modern — has prevailed until our own day.

Such was the state of scholarly opinion about the fall of Rome when Gibbon began his intensive study of the problem. He derived much aid from the seventeenth-century *érudits* whose ponderous tomes he had known and studied ever since his early Lausanne days and to defend whom he had written his *Essai sur l'étude de la littérature.* From them he acquired the vast learning and the scholarly regard for thoroughness and accuracy for which he is famous. If they had not laboriously assembled the ancient texts relevant to the various events of which he wrote, he could not have written his History. But Gibbon had no desire to become a mere *érudit* himself, living alone in an ivory tower, writing only for other scholars, and caring nothing for the good or bad opinion of the unlettered. His models, as a historian, were Robertson and Hume, and like them and the French *philosophes* whom he criticized for their unscholarly superficiality, he wanted his books to be read by educated people everywhere. He therefore used the works of the *érudits* as much as possible, but he did not imitate them.

CHAPTER SEVEN

GIBBON WRITES THE HISTORY

SOON after dropping his plans for a history of Switzerland, Gibbon began assembling materials for a history of the decline and fall of the Roman Empire. He had already carefully studied the Latin historians of the classic period — Sallust, Livy, and Tacitus, and the minor writers as well — and he had written brief essays about several of them. He now turned to the writers of the later period — Dio, the Augustan History, Ammianus, and a host of others — and during the last four years of his servitude to Buriton he worked his way through them until he 'almost grasped the ruins of Rome in the fourteenth Century, without suspecting that this final chapter must be attained by the labour of six quartos and twenty years'.[1]

During these last years at Buriton Gibbon also studied the works of several *érudits*. The list of these writers is long, but first and foremost among them stood the French le Nain de Tillemont (1637–98). This austere Jansenist had devoted his life to collecting, criticizing, and arranging whatever the ancients had written about the history of the first six centuries of the Roman Empire. Gibbon had read a few chapters of his *Histoire des empereurs* while in the militia, and he cited him frequently in the notes to *The Decline and Fall*. But though he used Tillemont freely he also laughed at him, calling him a 'learned compiler', and 'the patient and surefooted mule of the Alps', but also 'that incomparable guide, whose bigotry is overbalanced by the merits of erudition, diligence, veracity, and scrupulous minuteness'.[2] The *Annali* and *Antiquitates* of Muratori (1672–1750) were Gibbon's principal guide to the medieval period, and the German Mosheim (1694–1755) was his chief authority for Church history. He supplemented these writers with the *Annales Ecclesiastici* of Cardinal Baronius (1538–1607), of whom Gibbon remarked that he had 'sunk to the lowest degree of credulity which was compatible with learning'.

'At the outset', Gibbon recalls in his Memoirs, 'all was dark and doubtful — even the title of the work, the true æra of the decline and fall of the Empire, the limits of the Introduction, the division of the chapters, and the order of the narrative.' A more definite picture of Rome's decline presently began to emerge in his mind, however, and before he left Buriton he had settled upon the main outlines of his story. He had decided to write the history of the thirteen hundred years between the death of the Emperor Marcus Aurelius (A.D. 180) and the renaissance of arts and letters in the fifteenth century. He then divided Rome's long decline into three periods. The first would extend from 180 to 476, when Rome was 'subjected to the power of a Gothic conqueror'; the second, from 476 to 800, would cover the futile attempts of Justinian and Charlemagne to restore the Empire in the West; and the third would carry the story down to the capture of Constantinople by the Turks in 1453. When he came to write the History, however, this neat division into periods was drastically modified. The career of Charlemagne, for example, is not pictured as marking a turning-point in history: it is tucked away in the middle of a chapter dealing with a wide variety of matters. And in later years Gibbon regretted that he had begun his main narrative in 180: he thought that he should have 'deduced the decline of the Empire from the Civil Wars that ensued after the Fall of Nero [A.D. 68], or even from the tyranny which succeeded the reign of Augustus'.[3]

During his years at Buriton Gibbon also wrote a few preliminary sketches, two of which have survived. A footnote to *The Decline and Fall* mentions a 'rough draught of the present History' made 'as early as 1771', but Lord Sheffield found nothing among his friend's papers which he recognized as this preliminary sketch. It seems probable, however, that the manuscript which he published under the title, 'Outlines of the History of the World', had been a part of this early draft. In spite of its all-embracing title, the 'Outlines' deals only with the history of Europe and the Near East from 800 to 1500 — the period which Gibbon considered the third and last phase of Rome's decline and which he covered in his fifth and sixth volumes. Presumably the manuscript had once contained two other parts, in which the author summarized the history of the two earlier phases of Rome's decline (A.D. 180 to 476, and 476 to 800). At any rate the footnote in the History referring to the rough draft dealt with events which took place in the year 406.[4]

When composing the 'Outlines' Gibbon arranged events century by century and country by country, and he was sparing in his comments upon them. Nevertheless in these terse summaries we can distinguish many of his characteristic ideas. The fascination which the Orient always held for him is shown in countless passages dealing with the Byzantine emperors, the caliphs of Baghdad and Cordoba, the Crusaders, and Genghis Khan. He has much to say about liberty and despotism, but the liberty he praised is liberty for the upper classes only, for Gibbon never trusted the populace: 'Florence, like Athens, experienced all the evils incident, or rather inherent, to a wild democracy.' Likewise the author's hostility to the Church is often revealed: 'The numerous vermin of mendicant friars, who swarmed in this century, disgraced religion, learning, and common sense'; and Louis IX of France, 'notwithstanding he has been disgraced by the title of Saint, possessed uncommon virtues and abilities'.[5] Here again, as in his attack upon Bishop Warburton, Gibbon shows a pugnacity that is best explained by the general feeling of frustration under which he suffered during his last years at Buriton.

A very different spirit pervades the ten-page essay which Gibbon eventually appended to the third volume of his History. In this volume, published in March 1781, Gibbon traced the story of Rome's decline down to the end of its first phase in the year 476, and at its close he inserted this essay under the title, 'General Observations on the Fall of the Roman Empire in the West'. In these 'Observations' he drew a parallel between the Rome of the fifth century and the Europe of his own day: 'a Julian or Semiramis may reign in the North', he remarked, 'while Arcadius and Honorius again slumber on the thrones of the House of Bourbon'. When Louis XVI read, or heard of, this remark he resented its implications to such an extent that two years later, when Gibbon applied for a secretaryship at the British embassy in Paris, the king declared him *persona non grata*. Gibbon was able to boast of having incurred the royal displeasure. Nevertheless he changed 'the House of Bourbon' to 'the South' in the next edition of the History. In a note added to his Memoirs (evidently written late in 1792) Gibbon reported the affair and commented, 'I shall neither disclaim the allusion nor examine the likeness; but the situation of the *late* King of France excludes all suspicion of flattery, and I am ready to declare that the concluding observations of my third Volume were written before his accession to the throne.' Gibbon therefore must have composed the 'Observations' before May 1774.[6]

In the first half of this essay Gibbon briefly discussed what he then considered the causes of Rome's downfall. After firmly rejecting the suggestion that such calamities are to be attributed to Fortune, he developed the thesis that Rome's greatness had been due to the virtues — especially the military virtues — of her people, and that the loss of these virtues brought about her decline and fall by making it easy for the barbarians to overrun her provinces. He also blamed the 'immoderate greatness' of the Roman Empire, which led to a division of power between Constantinople and the West. And finally he laid much blame on the Christians, who turned men's thoughts and interest from this world to the next. Nevertheless he freely admitted that these Christians softened Rome's fall and preserved something of her culture. The remainder of the essay is devoted to a discussion of whether modern Europe should expect a similar decline and fall. Gibbon declared such a catastrophe to be impossible, and closed his essay with a brief confession of faith: 'We may therefore acquiesce in the pleasing conclusion that every age of the world has increased, and still increases, the real wealth, the happiness, the knowledge, and perhaps the virtue, of the human race.'

Though Gibbon thus seems to accept the eighteenth-century theory of progress as his guide through the misty maze of history, he did so only for a moment. This doctrine of universal progress was the creation of the French *philosophes*, of whom he had been critical ever since his first stay in Lausanne, when he planned and wrote the first pages of his *Essai sur l'étude de la littérature*. The theme of his History, and even its title, show his fundamental antipathy to the French doctrine, and his momentary acceptance of it is evidence of a happy frame of mind in 1772 and 1773. Gibbon was no longer pugnacious towards the world in general. He was gaining recognition in the literary society of London, and he saw a rosy future lying open before him. No wonder the human race seemed to be progressing.

Early in 1773, as soon as he had established himself and his library in London, Gibbon began writing the History, and in the summer of 1774, as the manuscript of his first volume was approaching completion, he made arrangements with a distinguished publisher, Thomas Cadell, for its publication.[7] Gibbon's successes in London's literary and political circles at just this time brought so many interruptions, however, that the manuscript was not ready for the printer until June 1775. But on 1 August he was able to report to Holroyd that 'The head is now printing, true: but it was writ last year and the year before, the first Chapter has been composed *de nouveau three times*; the second *twice* and all the others have undergone reviews, corrections &c. As to the tail it is perfectly formed and digested (and were I so much given to self content and haste) it is almost all written. The ecclesiastical part for instance is written out in fourteen sheets, which I mean to refondre from beginning to end.' At long last, however, the great day arrived and, as he notified Deyverdun, 'I gave myself to the Universe, and the Universe received me with open arms.' The first volume of Gibbon's *Decline and Fall of the Roman Empire* was published on 17 February 1776.[8]

Cadell declared later that the book had sold 'like a three penny pamphlet on current affairs', and that 'within a fortnight not a single copy remained'. He had originally planned to print 750 copies of the book but, on second thought, he reduced the number to 500. After the first half of the book had been printed, however, he changed his mind once more and decided to print 1000 copies, even though this decision required him to reset the type for the part already printed. A second edition of 1500 copies was published in June 1776, and a third edition of 1000 copies followed in May 1777. Nevertheless the demand for the book was so great that the book pirates of Dublin hastened to publish a cheap and unauthorized edition in 1776.[9]

This first volume of *The Decline and Fall* falls into three distinct parts: in the first three chapters Gibbon gives us a brilliant picture of the Roman Empire as he conceived it to have been in the second century after Christ; the next eleven chapters trace the political and military history of that Empire from the accession of Commodus (A.D. 180) to the end of the civil wars under Constantine (A.D. 324); and the last two chapters (xv and xvi) contain his famous account of early Christianity. This third section has always been the most widely read, the most discussed, and perhaps the most influential part of the book, but for us the first section is the most important. In these first three chapters we find most of what is essential in Gibbon.

The attentive reader of *The Decline and Fall* soon notices that, even when writing learnedly about ancient Rome, Gibbon usually has one eye fixed on the exciting world around him and that many oblique references to contemporary events have found their way into his text or notes. Occasionally these references are quite explicit, but more commonly they take the form of vague allusions or suggested parallels between ancient and modern times, with the reader left to guess the modern half of the equation. Thus, in the instance quoted above, Gibbon certainly considered Frederick the Great and Catherine of Russia the modern counterparts of Julian and Semiramis though he named neither of them. Gibbon saw a fundamental similarity between second-century Rome and eighteenth-century England, and in his first three chapters he elaborated upon those features of the Roman Empire that, he believed, should be admired by good British Whigs. Imperial Rome therefore takes on the semblance of an idealized and Whiggish version of imperial England in the happy years that lay between the Treaty of Paris (1763) and the outbreak of the American Revolution in 1775.

The famous opening sentence of Gibbon's History announced sententiously that 'In the second century of the Christian Æra, the empire of Rome comprehended the fairest part of the earth, and the most civilized portion of mankind.' The peoples of this vast empire were blessed with freedom, peace, and prosperity; they were united by laws, and in general their rulers were wise, simple, and beneficent. The vicious emperors of the first century whom Tacitus had consigned to everlasting infamy — 'the dark, unrelenting Tiberius, the furious Caligula, the stupid Claudius, the profligate and cruel Nero, the beastly Vitellius, and the inhuman Domitian' — had been succeeded by the five 'Good Emperors' of the second century — Nerva, Trajan, Hadrian, Antoninus Pius, and Marcus Aurelius. These five men presided over what Gibbon regarded as Rome's Golden Age. He pictured this age as one in which economic progress was shared by the citizens of countless beautiful and prosperous cities. Commerce was aided by the Roman peace, the imperial roads and post, and the great demand for the new luxuries from the East, while agriculture was improved until 'the beautiful face of the country [was] cultivated and adorned like an immense garden'. It was a period of general felicity and, as Gibbon remarked, 'If a man were called to fix the period in the history of the world during which the condition of the human race was most happy and prosperous, he would, without hesitation, name that which elapsed from the death of Domitian [A.D. 96] to the accession of Commodus [A.D. 180].'[10]

Gibbon opened his account of this magnificent century with a eulogy of Trajan, the last of the great Roman conquerors. He described his hero's military successes in Dacia, Asia Minor, and Parthia, and he reported, with great though perhaps understandable exaggeration, that 'Every day the astonished senate received the intelligence of new names and new nations that acknowledged his sway.' Reading this passage must have reminded many of Gibbon's contemporaries of their own experiences in the famous 'year of victories' (1759), when, in the course of a few months, they received the astonishing news of British victories at Minden and Guadeloupe, Quebec and Quiberon Bay, coming not long after Clive's victory at Plassey and quickly followed by that at Wandiwash. Gibbon had shared in the excitement of the time, and perhaps he bore it in mind as he wrote this page in his History. And when he declared that at this time 'the Roman name was revered among the most remote nations of the earth', he may well have recalled for a moment the reverence accorded the British name in Paris — upon which he commented during his first visit to that city immediately after the Peace of 1763.[11]

Gibbon's account of second-century Rome emphasized the liberty which, he believed, had then been enjoyed by the enlightened upper classes throughout the Empire. This liberty he called 'rational freedom', and it was neither freedom for the 'wild democracy' nor was it 'savage independence'. It was liberty as liberty was understood by an eighteenth-century British Whig. Gibbon believed that rational liberty of this sort had prevailed at Rome under the Republic, that Augustus had artfully undermined it, and that the Good Emperors had restored and preserved it — at least in its essentials — in spite of the blows it had received during the turmoil of the last century of the Republic and the first century of the Empire. The Roman Senate was the palladium of this liberty: as long as the Senate remained powerful, Rome was 'free', and whoever attacked the Senate attacked liberty itself. This was good Whig doctrine, and if we bear in mind that in 1773 and 1774, when Gibbon was writing these pages, he and his friends were anxiously trying to persuade his cousin Eliot to give the historian a seat in Parliament, perhaps it will help us to understand his reverence for the Roman Senate.

This Roman liberty, which so aroused Gibbon's enthusiasm, was enjoyed by all Roman citizens throughout their vast Empire. Citizenship had at one time been limited to free men living in the city itself or in its immediate vicinity, but before the end of the Republic its rights were enjoyed by all free-born Italians. During the first two centuries of the Empire citizenship was gradually extended to provincials until it was shared by the middle and upper classes everywhere. In Gibbon's view the social and political position of these Roman citizens was not very different from that of the upper middle class in England in his day — the class to which he himself belonged. The officials of the Roman Empire, who were its actual rulers, came from this class, and many men of provincial origin occupied high posts in the government. 'The grandsons of the Gauls who had besieged Julius Caesar in Alesia', wrote Gibbon, 'commanded legions, governed provinces, and were admitted into the senate at Rome. Their ambition, instead of disturbing the tranquillity of the state, was intimately connected with its safety and greatness.' Moreover the historian could find no traces at Rome of that racism which, he believed, had hastened the ruin of Athens and Sparta.[12]

Gibbon was equally pleased with the broad religious toleration practised throughout the Roman Empire, attributing it to indifference and a decline of superstition and religious fanaticism. 'The various modes of worship which prevailed in the Roman world were all considered by the people as equally true; by the philosopher as equally false; and by the magistrate as equally useful.'[13] Gibbon optimistically believed that the same indifference regarding religion prevailed in England in his own day, but he was presently chagrined to learn that it did not.

Gibbon opened his discussion of Rome's colonial policy with a brief account of how the Romans founded colonies in Italy, in the western provinces of Gaul and Spain, and even in Asia Minor. At first the colonists were soldiers, sent to hold and defend the newly conquered territories, but each colony was a little Rome, a centre for the diffusion of the Latin language and the Roman way of life. David Hume had suggested this interpretation of the influence of Roman colonies to Gibbon as early as 1767, and Gibbon mentioned it in his 'General Observations' a few years later.[14] In each case the author specifically mentioned the English colonies in America as following the Roman pattern, and Gibbon spoke of 'the American world which is already filled with [Europe's] colonies and institutions'. It was with ideas such as these in his mind that Gibbon composed the first volume of his History.

Though he found much to admire in the Roman Empire of the second century, Gibbon's apprehensions were aroused by weaknesses which he detected in the imperial system. Roman citizens might still consider themselves free men, but the days of their freedom were numbered and the foundations of tyranny had been laid by Augustus, the founder of the Empire (27 B.C. – A.D. 14). Gibbon devoted several pages to the schemings of that 'crafty tyrant' and his sly efforts to gain absolute power. Augustus was not successful in his efforts to establish an autocracy, but there was always the danger that, though he failed, one of his successors might succeed. The Good Emperors were not afflicted by this ambition to tyranny, but even in their day patriotic Romans 'must often have recollected the instability of a happiness which depended on the character of a single man'.[15] When writing these pages Gibbon may have been thinking not only of the Roman Augustus, but also of the British George III. George was often accused of trying to make himself a despot, and Gibbon's Whig friends frequently described their king in terms resembling those that the historian applied to Augustus.

A second element of weakness in the Empire was to be found, according to Gibbon, in Rome's military system. During his years of service in the militia Gibbon had made a careful study of the Roman army, listing in his Journal the ancient and modern writers whom he consulted. Some of the latter he praised, but he expressed his contempt for others — 'mere scholars who perhaps had never seen a battalion under arms'.[16] Now, slightly more than ten years later, he incorporated the fruits of these early researches in his History, and to them he added various remarks on the social and political aspects of Rome's military policies. In the days of the Republic, he pointed out, the Roman army had been an army of citizens 'who had a country to love, a property to defend, and some share in enacting' the laws under which they lived. But in the days of the Empire, 'war was gradually improved into an art and degraded into a trade'. 'The common soldiers, like the mercenary troops of modern Europe, were drawn from the meanest, and very frequently the most profligate, of mankind.'[17] Montesquieu had expressed similar views concerning the Roman army, but in defending the militia against the mercenaries Gibbon was not following the French philosopher; he was speaking as a captain of the Hampshire militia.

The disastrous consequences of this change to an army of professionals are shown by Gibbon a few chapters later. During years of peace these idle mercenaries wanted something to do and were therefore ready to follow any leader who would pay them well. With their aid Septimius Severus seized the throne in A.D. 193, for which reason 'posterity justly considered him the principal author of the decline of the Roman Empire'.[18]

Still more ominous, according to Gibbon, was the indolence into which men fell when the Government did everything for them. They enjoyed a debilitating love of luxury and ease; they lost their old-time courage and public spirit; and their resulting loss of liberty led to a general decline of culture. 'The name of Poet was almost forgotten; that of Orator was usurped by the sophists. A cloud of critics, of compilers, of commentators, darkened the face of learning, and the decline of genius was soon followed by the corruption of taste.... The Roman world was indeed populated by a race of pigmies when the fierce giants of the north broke in and mended the puny breed. They restored a manly spirit of freedom; and, after the revolution of ten centuries, freedom became the happy parent of taste and science.'[19]

The central chapters of Gibbon's first volume discuss Rome's misfortunes during the critical third century when the symptoms of decline were daily becoming more visible throughout the Empire. The licentious emperors were unable to defeat the barbarians, and they disregarded or oppressed the Senate. In the last years of the third century and early in the fourth, Diocletian and Constantine drastically reformed the government of the Empire, thereby saving it from immediate collapse, but the conversion of Constantine to Christianity brought new troubles. Gibbon developed this theme at length in his two long chapters on early Christianity.

These famous chapters open with a famous example of Gibbonian irony. After inquiring what were the means by which 'the Christian faith obtained so remarkable a victory over the established religions of the earth', the author replied,

> to this inquiry an obvious but satisfactory answer may be returned: that it was owing to the convincing evidence of the doctrine itself, and to the ruling providence of its great Author. But, as truth and reason seldom find so favourable a reception in the world, and as the wisdom of Providence frequently condescends to use the passions of the human heart, and the general circumstances of mankind, as instruments to execute its purpose; we may still be permitted, though with becoming submission, to ask not indeed what were the first, but what were the secondary causes of the rapid growth of the Christian church.

He then enumerated five such 'secondary' causes: the intolerant zeal of the Christians, their doctrine of a future life, their claim to miraculous powers, their pure and austere morals, and their union and discipline.

Long before he composed these chapters, Gibbon had decided that the historian must study Christianity in the same detached way that he would study any other religion, and by now he had become so habituated to this principle that he assumed everyone thought as he did about it. He was therefore surprised (and at first a little frightened) by the uproar these two chapters occasioned. Critics pounced upon the five 'secondary' causes, declaring that they could not explain the rapid expansion of Christianity. The critics would not have been satisfied, however, if Gibbon had added five more — or fifty more — causes of the same secular sort. They insisted that the victory of Christianity be ascribed to divine intervention, and this Gibbon could not, or would not, do. As long as critics limited themselves to attacks on his theology he merely smiled at their rantings, but questioning his scholarship was a different matter. When a brash young man from Oxford named Davis published a pamphlet accusing him of bad faith and deliberate misrepresentation, Gibbon replied with a blistering *Vindication*. Thereafter no one ventured to impugn his scholarship, and his critics limited themselves to indignant denunciations of his remarks about some of the early Christians and the irony and sarcasm with which he discussed miracles and other features of popular Christianity.[20]

The first volume of *The Decline and Fall* was scarcely off the press when Gibbon began work on the second. Late in June 1776 he wrote to Holroyd,[21] reporting that he was deeply engaged in the reign of Constantine, but complaining that his progress was delayed by his many distractions. His social life was the cause of many of these interruptions; others were due to his political activities; he spent several months in France in 1777; at the end of 1778 he devoted several weeks to writing his one and only reply to critics of his first volume (*A Vindication of . . . the XVth and XVIth Chapters*, published early in 1779); and in July and August 1779 he was busy with the *Mémoire justificatif*, in which he defended British policies towards France. Nevertheless he delivered the manuscript of the second and third volumes of his History to the printer in May 1780, and the two volumes were published on 1 March 1781.

Gibbon wrote the greater part of these two volumes between October 1777 and May 1780. Parliamentary opposition to George III and Lord North was then reaching its height, while the American Revolution was tearing the British Empire to pieces, and Gibbon could not remain untouched by the prevailing excitement. What he had heard from Burke in Parliament during the afternoon, and from Fox at the coffee-houses in the evening, was still vivid in his mind as he wrote about Rome the next morning. So many Whig ideas thus found their way into his narrative that these two volumes may be called a Whig version of the decline and fall of Rome. In them Gibbon maintains that the decline of Rome was due primarily to the despotism inherent in Constantine's system and to the spirit of faction which spread over the Empire. He attributes much of this faction to the Christians, but he treats such churchmen as Athanasius and Ambrose as heroes when they defy their despotic emperors. Above all these heroes, however, towers the Emperor Julian, whom he pictures as vainly attempting to unite the factions, to bring back the old free system, and to establish a rational religion. But even Julian was far from perfect: his zeal for the old gods of paganism made him intolerant and led him to commit grave injustices against the Christians.[22]

Shortly after the publication of these two volumes, Gibbon wrote to his stepmother that 'the Clergy (such is the advantage of total loss of character) commend my decency and moderation: but the patriots wish to damn the work and the Author'. The reason for this patriotic hostility to Gibbon is not far to seek. After associating with the Whigs for several years he had accepted a place under Lord North in 1779, thereby alienating Fox and his followers.

These former friends now ransacked his History for evidences of the author's perfidy and they found many passages which, they suggested, had been written while he was still an independent Member of Parliament, but which he had neglected to expunge after he became a placeman. Such passages deplored the neglect of the Senate, the progress of tyranny, and the decline of the military, and they often referred covertly to the American rebels. Two of the more obvious of these passages, describing conditions in the West in the fifth century, read as follows:

> Britain was irrecoverably lost. But, as the emperors wisely acquiesced in the independence of a remote province, the separation was not embittered by the reproach of tyranny or rebellion; and the claims of allegiance and protection were succeeded by the mutual and voluntary offices of national friendship.
>
> The Roman government appeared every day less formidable to its enemies, more odious and oppressive to its subjects. The taxes were multiplied with the public distress; economy was neglected in proportion as it became necessary; and the injustice of the rich shifted the unequal burden from themselves to the people, whom they defrauded of the *indulgencies* that might sometimes have alleviated their misery. The severe inquisition, which confiscated their goods and tortured their persons, compelled the subjects of Valentinian to prefer the more simple tyranny of the Barbarians, to fly to the woods and mountains, or to embrace the vile and abject condition of mercenary servants. They abjured and abhorred the name of Roman citizens, which had formerly excited the ambition of mankind. The Armorican provinces of Gaul, and the greatest part of Spain, were thrown into a state of disorderly independence, by the confederations of the Bagaudae; and the Imperial ministers pursued with proscriptive laws, and ineffectual arms, the rebels whom they had made. If all the Barbarian conquerors had been annihilated in the same hour, their total destruction would not have restored the empire of the West; and, if Rome still survived, she survived the loss of freedom, of virtue, and of honour.[23]

The first of these passages comes near the end of a long chapter detailing the horrors of the barbarian invasions of Italy, and it repeats ideas that Gibbon had expressed to his stepmother during the dark days following Burgoyne's surrender at Saratoga. The second passage is largely a free translation of Salvian (a Christian historian who lived in the fifth century), but it expresses the Whig party line against Lord North's Government so accurately that it is difficult not to believe that Gibbon was watching America as he wrote. This belief is strengthened by an interesting event that occurred in Parliament on 12 December 1781 — ten months after the second and third volumes of *The Decline and Fall* were published and barely two weeks after news reached London of Lord Cornwallis's surrender at Yorktown. A member of the Opposition moved in Parliament that no more efforts be made to subdue the rebellious colonies by force of arms. A member named Powys rose to second the motion and read this passage from Gibbon to the House.[24] The motion was never brought to a vote, but Powys showed that he had found in Gibbon support for his programme regarding the American colonies.

Another statesman to find succour in Gibbon's History was an American, Henry Laurens of South Carolina. Laurens had been president of the Continental Congress in 1778, and in August 1780 he was sent to Europe to negotiate a treaty with the Netherlands. The British captured him on the high seas, however, and incarcerated him in the Tower of London. After about a year his case came to the attention of Edmund Burke, who arranged that he be exchanged for Lord Cornwallis early in 1782.[25] In the summer of 1781, while in the Tower, Laurens read Gibbon's History (the second and third volumes of which had recently appeared) and marked and commented upon many passages which seemed to him to be critical of British policy. He copied out these passages and comments and sent the manuscript to Burke, who circulated it among his friends in Parliament and even urged Laurens to have it printed. Since Laurens was still in the Tower, he probably was wise to refuse. The story was not yet quite finished, however, for when Gibbon withdrew to Switzerland in September 1783 he and Laurens were two of the three passengers aboard the ship in which they crossed the Channel. Gibbon reported to Lord Sheffield that Laurens had read '*the* pamphlet' (referring to Sheffield's recent tract on American commerce) 'and thinks it has done much mischief, a good sign!' Seasickness then rendered further conversation between the fellow travellers difficult.[26]

Three months after Gibbon delivered the manuscript of the second and third volumes of his History to the printer, in May 1780, Eliot withdrew his favour and Gibbon lost his seat in Parliament. His enemies had been attacking him viciously ever since his appointment to the Board of Trade, and this was their culminating blow. In his discouragement Gibbon thought of concluding his History with the third volume and seeking more remunerative employment. A sentence in the preface to his second volume (dated 1 March 1781) expresses these doubts about continuing his History,[27] and for a full year thereafter he wrote nothing. He finally made up his mind to persevere, however, and in March 1782 he announced that he would continue the story down to the fall of Constantinople in 1453. Further troubles soon descended upon the unhappy historian. Within a few days came the fall of Lord North's ministry; in the following July Burke's Reform Bill of 1782 abolished the Board of Trade; and Gibbon thus lost his salary of £750. A year later he gave up the struggle and withdrew to Switzerland (September 1783).

It was during these difficult years of 1782 and 1783, when he was losing his income and England was losing America, that Gibbon wrote the greater part of his fourth volume. This volume was his answer to defeat. It is devoted largely to the Emperor Justinian, the strong monarch who surmounted the troubles of his time and reconquered much of what his predecessors had lost. Gibbon drew a brilliant and sympathetic picture of Justinian, which he supplemented with a few reflections of a deeper sort. In the long run he decided, Justinian's military victories were of little avail and his glory rests on a far greater achievement: England, too, should rest her case on something more permanent than military victory.

Gibbon then wrote the most widely praised chapter of his History — the one dealing with the 'fair and everlasting monument' of the Justinian code. This legal system was Rome's great contribution to the world, and because of it men 'piously commemorate [Justinian's] virtues; dissemble or deny his failings; and fiercely chastise the guilt or folly of the rebels who presume to sully the majesty of the purple'.[28] Gibbon thus expressed his belief that the British system of liberty and tolerance, about which he spoke so often and so eloquently, might, like the Roman law, be a lasting boon to mankind. And who were those rebels who had presumed 'to sully the majesty of the purple'? Some may have lived in the sixth century, it is true, but one of them was named George Washington. Such, at any rate, was the view of the discouraged British historian in 1783.

The fifth and sixth volumes of *The Decline and Fall*, which were composed at Lausanne between July 1784 and June 1787, differ markedly from their predecessors. This is partly because the first four volumes give a detailed account of the history of about four and a half centuries, while the last two volumes cover nearly eight hundred years. Gibbon did not know the period so well or have such good guides to the source material as he did for the early volumes, but more important was his mental state. Not only had he been exhausted by the nervous tension under which he lived during his last years in London, but at Lausanne he found a very different and much less stimulating intellectual atmosphere. Lausanne society had no conversationalists equal to Fox or Burke, Dr. Johnson or Horace Walpole — or Gibbon himself. In fact there was no one in Lausanne with whom he could converse on equal terms.

Moreover Gibbon had lost his interest in English political life.

Three months after he left England, the 'infamous coalition' of Fox and North fell from power, and the younger Pitt, then twenty-four years of age, entered upon his celebrated ministry. The old factions were overcome, and the new prime minister led England in that remarkable national revival which made possible her twenty years of war against France and Napoleon. It might seem that this new Government fulfilled Gibbon's ancient wish for a national ministry, and that a Justinian had arisen in England. But Gibbon could not enjoy Pitt's triumphant progress. The statesmen in power were no longer those friends of his who, in various permutations and combinations, had ruled England for so many years. A new group had rallied around the youthful Pitt, and among them was one whom Gibbon knew only too well — his cousin Eliot, now Lord Eliot and father-in-law of the prime minister's sister. The historian grumbled that England was being governed by boys and turned his attention to his History.

The resulting fifth and sixth volumes of *The Decline and Fall* started badly. The first chapter of the fifth volume (chapter xlviii) is the worst in the book. The author confines himself to chronicling 'the revolutions of the [Byzantine] throne, the successions of families, the personal characters of the Greek princes, the mode of their life and death, the maxims and influence of their domestic government, and the tendency of their reign to accelerate or suspend the downfall of the Eastern empire'. In the seventy pages of this chapter he summarizes the reigns of more than fifty emperors. The dullness of this chapter and the next are best explained by their author's nervous exhaustion resulting from the strain under which he had lived during his last years in London. He gradually regained his strength, however, and his concluding volumes contain some of his most brilliant writing. The exigencies of his narrative now carried him to the East, where the story centres in Constantinople. We follow the fortunes of a varied host of peoples, Greeks and Arabs, Franks and Normans, Slavs and Hungarians, Mohammed and Saladin, Genghis Khan and Tamerlane, Paleologue and

Mohammed II. We feel the romance of the Orient, and at the same time we know that the Byzantines are defending civilization against uncultured peoples whom they will eventually civilize. And, at the very end, we see Greek learning brought from Constantinople to Italy and the rebirth of Western culture during the Renaissance. In drawing vivid pictures of these events Gibbon was at his best: his literary style had achieved its perfection; his mind was at ease, his temper reminiscent, his imagination colourful and brilliant. Everything conspired to make these chapters a fitting crown for the historian's life-work.

CHAPTER EIGHT

EDWARD GIBBON THE HISTORIAN

READERS of Gibbon's *History of the Decline and Fall of the Roman Empire* will be disappointed if they expect to find in it a closely reasoned philosophical or sociological treatise on the causes of Rome's collapse. Nowhere in his six volumes does he make a full and explicit statement of what, in his opinion, were the great determining causes of that catastrophe. He does not even discuss such elementary but fundamental questions as the meaning of the word 'fall', and exactly what fell. Only in a few paragraphs of the brief 'General Observations', appended to his third volume, does he broach the subject of why Rome fell, and his sketchy remarks on that occasion should not be taken as expressing the historian's mature views on the matter. Unfortunately, however, modern commentators sometimes forget this fact and, on the basis of a few sentences in this excursus, they ascribe to Gibbon ideas which he held only momentarily if at all.

But though Gibbon made no effort to find a neat and brief formula that would adequately explain the actions of many millions of people over a period of several centuries, he occasionally let drop a casual remark to the effect that this or that event or policy, which he had just described, contributed to the ruin of the Roman Empire. These remarks are not based on any consistent theory of historical development, yet they give us valuable hints as to what their author was thinking as he wrote.

Like many of his contemporaries Gibbon saw a close parallel between the Roman Empire of antiquity and the British Empire of his own day, and in his History he ascribed to ancient Rome not only the glories of the British Empire, but also its weaknesses. He deplored Rome's loss of liberty and the ever-increasing power of the emperors, their disregard of the Senate, the loss of whole provinces, and the pernicious bigotry of the Christian sects. These same misfortunes, or something very like them, seemed to threaten the British Empire in Gibbon's own day, as Whig orators and journalists were constantly pointing out in their attacks upon Lord North and his ministry.

Gibbon did not take an active part in this great struggle, but countless passages in his History show that he could not escape emotional involvement. 'Liberty' had always been one of his watchwords, and he believed that all culture and civilization itself were dependent upon it. As a boy in Lausanne he wrote to a professor at Zürich saying, 'The cause of literature indeed stands by freedom.' And a few years later, during his second stay at Lausanne, he attributed Lausanne's cultural backwardness to her lack of liberty.[1] This same idea pervades *The Decline and Fall.* As Roman liberty declined, her culture and civilization declined as well. He even declares that 'when the fierce giants of the north broke in, they restored a manly spirit of freedom; and, after the revolution of ten centuries, freedom became the happy parent of taste and science'.[2]

At the end of an especially doleful chapter on Rome's misfortunes in the fifth century Gibbon sadly remarked that 'if Rome still survived, she survived the loss of freedom, of virtue, and of honour'.[3] These terms are very slippery, and nowhere does Gibbon accurately define them, but apparently he used them as a summary of those habits and intellectual and moral patterns that underlie civilized life and without which such life is impossible. In these three vague words he summarized what we today call the *mores*, or 'way of life', of a people. Any relaxation of the power of these *mores* over the individual would lead inevitably to social decline, and such decline would lead in turn to a further weakening of the *mores*. Gibbon apparently believed that, in the final analysis, the fall of

Rome was caused by this 'loss of freedom, of virtue, and of honour'. Or, as he put it in another chapter, the virtuous Romans of the old school (who still retained freedom, virtue, and honour) were supplanted by 'barbarian invaders who were strangers to the laws, the language, and the religion, of the Romans'.[4] The resulting change in *mores* was the real 'fall of Rome'.

Countless other passages show Gibbon as a moralist, and sometimes they make the History itself seem like an eloquent and impressive sermon. Gibbon certainly was no Pietist, and his History bears little resemblance to the sermons of John Wesley or the writings of William Law, yet it shows how deeply he was concerned with moral values. In his Journal he often commented favourably on the sermons he heard at Buriton or Paris or Lausanne, but his growing scepticism turned him away from the churches and led him to develop the secular morality which he summarized in the words, 'freedom, virtue, and honour'.

In clarifying his ideas on this subject Gibbon was much influenced by the Roman historians, who, as we have seen, usually gave their histories a highly moralistic turn. At times Sallust and Tacitus became quite lurid in their descriptions and denunciations of decadent Rome, as did the poet Juvenal, whom Gibbon read with especial delight during his crucial stay at Lausanne in 1763. The influence of these Roman moralists is evident on many a page of *The Decline and Fall*: for example, it might seem that Sallust's unforgettable paragraph about Sempronia, the noble lady who took part in the Catalinarian conspiracy, had inspired Gibbon's portraits of more than one Roman empress — or, if we disregard chronology, we might say that Sempronia seems to step from the pages of *The Decline and Fall*. Like Sallust and Juvenal, Gibbon sought to turn men from vice, not by making it odious but by making it ridiculous.

As Gibbon's awe-inspiring picture of Rome's decline could impress nearly anyone, many readers who deeply deplored his attitude towards organized religion recognized his value as a moral tonic. In 1826 the ridiculous Bowdler published an edition of *The Decline and Fall* 'with careful omission of all passages of an irreligious or immoral tendency', and managed to salvage five volumes of edification. It was this moralizing aspect of Gibbon that Charles Dickens saw fit to ridicule in *Our Mutual Friend*, but there were many people in nineteenth-century England whose intellectual endowments were greater than those of Silas Wegg and Mr. and Mrs. Boffin, but who found their morale fortified by the contemplation of Gibbon's tremendous spectacle. *The Decline and Fall of the Roman Empire* became an active moral force in Victorian England.

It might also be said that Gibbon exercised a noticeable influence on the political life of England in the nineteenth century. Many of the political principles that he approved were widely popular with Englishmen throughout that century — liberty, parliamentary government, religious toleration, humanitarianism, and the like. Gibbon praised these cardinal principles in stately periods, and he made it seem that all history supported his belief that the world's mightiest empire had fallen because the Romans had disregarded or violated these precepts. Many educated leaders of England in the nineteenth century esteemed Gibbon highly — Gladstone is reliably reported to have ranked him third among the world's great historians, preceded only by Thucydides and Fra Paolo Sarpi — and his admirers sometimes regarded him as an oracle. They were impressed by his demonstration of the strength of their principles, and their faith in these principles was thereby quickened.

Several of England's great empire-builders of the period confessed their admiration of Gibbon and acknowledged their indebtedness to him. By reading his History they came upon ideas which they attempted to realize in the British Empire. Cecil Rhodes is said to have admired Gibbon 'to the point of idolatry', and Gibbon's influence on the young Winston Churchill has been widely recognized. In general, however, Gibbon's influence on British imperialism was more subtle. He wrote about the decline of the Western Empire just as Britain was losing America, and his narrative then carried him to the East, where something of the Roman Empire remained. There is no evidence that Gibbon ever imagined that India might compensate England for the loss of her American colonies, or even that his History suggested this idea to others. But his glowing account of the Byzantine Empire draws the reader's attention to the East, where, just beyond the horizon, lies India. Moreover, the heroes of these two last volumes are apt to resemble Englishmen in India, or else those Oriental grandees against whom they fought. In his vivid pictures of the Orient Gibbon indirectly does something of what Kipling did in a more direct way a hundred years later. In his last two volumes it is possible to catch a vague foreshadowing of the 'White Man's Burden' and 'dominion over palm and pine'.

The varying fortunes of the two notorious chapters on early Christianity are especially interesting and significant in this regard. After the first uproar had subsided, Gibbon admitted that they were bound to 'create many enemies and conciliate few friends'. This judgement was certainly correct. Ecclesiastical writers rushed to the defence of their Church, while those who admired the book ignored the offending chapters. Early in the nineteenth century a few free spirits derived pleasure from the contemplation of Gibbon 'sapping a solemn creed with solemn sneer', but most of his admirers continued to deplore his infidelity. Towards the middle of the century, however, this attitude began to change. A sceptical spirit spread among the thinking classes in England, and many a youthful atheist found his most courageous doubts confirmed by reading Gibbon's fifteenth and sixteenth chapters. They became a widely read portion of the book, and sometimes, perhaps, the mere reputation of these chapters fortified the doubts of eager sceptics who had no time to read them.

Gibbon owed much to the *érudits* who preceded him, and he freely acknowledged his indebtedness to them ('my narrative was deduced from the last period of Classical reading', he wrote in his Memoirs[5]), but he did not share the Mandarinism which caused these scholars to write primarily for their colleagues. He had been led to history by Robertson and Hume and, like his masters, he wrote for the educated public. His brilliant literary powers and his wit assured that he would be read; his amazing accuracy put him beyond the reach of pettifogging mistake-finders; his book quickly became a classic, and such it has remained to the present day; but it is not a reference book, to be consulted and quoted as an authority for the facts of history. Almost two hundred years of research have greatly extended our knowledge of Roman history, but as a literary historian Gibbon remains supreme.

In his youthful *Essai sur l'étude de la littérature* Gibbon had expressed the view that the works of poets and scholars could be of service to their country, and had gone to quite absurd lengths in attempting to prove his contention by showing how Virgil's *Georgics* had helped Augustus. In his mature years he did not labour this thesis so ardently, but neither did he surrender it. Countless passages in his notes, or even in the text itself, refer obliquely or directly to contemporary events in an urbanely polemical spirit. Gibbon wrote a vivid account of what should, in his opinion, be expected whenever a whole people loses its freedom, its virtue, and its honour, and his big book exercised an observable influence upon the religious, and even the political, development of the next hundred years.

But Gibbon did not foresee these consequences of his life-work, nor did he intend them. He was not a fanatic, bursting with information which he believed everyone should have; he was not consciously trying to save the world; and only the French Revolution convinced him that it really needed saving. What he desired above all else was literary fame, and this he won. 'Fame', he wrote, 'is the motive, it is the reward, of our labours', and on another occasion he wrote to Lord Sheffield, 'I sometimes reflect with pleasure that my writings will survive me.'[6] His dream has been fulfilled and the fame he desired has been granted. In spite of — or perhaps because of — his sickly childhood and his unhappy youth, and in spite of the distractions of a London clubman and disillusioned Member of Parliament, this patient scholar, who preferred the difficult works of the humanists and *érudits* to those of the gay but superficial *philosophes*, wrote one of the world's great histories. He is still known as 'Edward Gibbon *the* Historian'.

KEY TO ABBREVIATIONS

EDITIONS OF GIBBON'S WORKS

DF. *The History of the Decline and Fall of the Roman Empire*, by Edward Gibbon (ed. J. B. Bury, 7 vols.). London, 1909–14.

References in the notes are to volume and page of this second Bury edition; references in the text are to the volumes in which they appeared in Gibbon's first edition (6 vols., 1776–88). Thus, the famous fifteenth and sixteenth chapters were in vol. I in the first edition, but in the notes they are assigned to Bury, II, 1–148.

Hill. *The Memoirs of the Life of Edward Gibbon* (ed. George Birkbeck Hill). London, 1900.

A reprint of Sheffield's edition, with many valuable notes.

JA. *Gibbon's Journal to January 28th, 1763* (ed. D. M. Low). London, 1929.

JB. *Le Journal de Gibbon à Lausanne, 17 août 1763–19 avril 1764* (ed. Georges Bonnard). Lausanne, 1945.

JC. *Gibbon's Journey from Geneva to Rome; His Journal from 20 April to 2 October 1764* (ed. Georges Bonnard). London, 1961.

L. *The Letters of Edward Gibbon* (ed. J. E. Norton, 3 vols.). London, 1956.

LP. *Private Letters of Edward Gibbon (1753–1794)* (ed. Rowland E. Prothero, 2 vols.). London, 1897.

Contains many letters to Gibbon not in Miss Norton's edition.

M. *The Autobiographies of Edward Gibbon* (ed. John Murray). London, 1896.

The six drafts, as written by Gibbon.

MG. *Miscellanea Gibboniana* (ed. Gavin R. de Beer, Georges A. Bonnard, Louis Junod). Lausanne, 1957.

MW. *The Miscellaneous Works of Edward Gibbon, Esq.* (ed. John, Lord Sheffield), 2nd edn. (5 vols.). London, 1814.

BOOKS ABOUT GIBBON

Harold L. Bond, *The Literary Art of Edward Gibbon.* Oxford, 1960.

Giuseppe Giarrizzo, *Edward Gibbon e la cultura europea del settecento.* Naples, 1954.

An ambitious work, based on wide reading.

Geoffrey Keynes, *The Library of Edward Gibbon.* Oxford, 1940.

D. M. Low, *Edward Gibbon, 1737–1794.* London, 1937.

The best biography.

S. T. McCloy, *Gibbon's Antagonism to Christianity and the Discussions that it has provoked.* London, 1933.

J. E. Norton, *A Bibliography of the Works of Edward Gibbon.* Oxford, 1940.

Meredith Read, *Historic Studies in Vaud, Berne & Savoy* (2 vols.). London, 1897.

This author, an American general with antiquarian tastes, has gathered many odds and ends about Gibbon at Lausanne.

G. M. Young, *Gibbon.* New York, 1933.

NOTES

CHAPTER ONE

1. M. 302, 333. By consulting the British Astronomer-Royal, Birkbeck Hill learned that, sure enough, the moon was shining on Lake Leman between the hours of eleven and twelve on the night of 27 June 1787. Hill, 331.

2. L. II, 386, 410, and others.

3. M. 356.

4. M. 6, 362; Shakespeare, *2 Henry VI*, IV, vii.

5. For Gibbon's book-plates see G. Keynes, *The Library of Edward Gibbon* (1940), 33–34.

6. See G. Bonnard, 'Gibbon at Work on his *Memoirs*', in *English Studies*, XLV, 209–13.

7. L. III, 246.

8. Note by Sheffield, M. 4 n.

9. British Museum, Add. MS. 36248, fo. 9.

CHAPTER TWO

1. We know Gibbon's mother, Judith Porten Gibbon, only from a few lines in his Memoirs, but as he was not yet ten years old when she died, he had only the vaguest recollections of her. He knew only what his father and aunt had told him. She apparently was a woman of domineering character and the socially ambitious member of the Gibbon family. She had raised her social standing considerably by her marriage, and she was determined to rise still farther, even if it entailed gross neglect of her sickly son. Gibbon declares that his health was so poor in childhood that his parents constantly feared for his life and therefore gave each of their other sons the name Edward to make sure that this family name would be perpetuated in case of his death. This statement is incorrect, for the other children were given Porten names; one son was named James Edward, it is true, but two others were baptized simply James (after Mrs. Gibbon's father), one was named Stanier (after her brother), one was William (not a family name in either family), and their one daughter was given her own name, Judith. Mrs. Gibbon obviously dominated the family at Putney. See the genealogical table in Low, *Edward Gibbon*, 352 ff., and in his introduction to JA. xxix.

2. M. 48; L. III, 46–47.
3. M. 59.
4. M. 63.
5. Quoted by Hill, 63 n.
6. M. 78.
7. MW. II, 37.
8. M. 63.
9. M. 79–80, 121.
10. M. 84.
11. M. 239.
12. This letter has been lost, but its general tenor may be gathered from Gibbon's report of it to Suzanne Curchod. L. I, 91.
13. JA. 72.
14. Dorothea Gibbon Papers (in Yale Library), III, fo. 4.
15. JA. 185.
16. JA. 22; M. 189; cf. JA. 193–5.
17. The official police report on this fracas has been published by Georges Bonnard as app. I of his edition of *Le Journal de Gibbon à Lausanne*, JB. 273–80.
18. JB. 58, 263.
19. Bonnard published many extracts from Guise's diary in his edition of *Gibbon's Journey from Geneva to Rome*.
20. L. I, 184; M. 267.
21. M. 271.
22. M. 274–5.
23. D. M. Low, *Edward Gibbon*, 359.
24. J. E. Norton, *A Bibliography of The Works of Edward Gibbon*, 177 n.

CHAPTER THREE

1. M. 207; for Holroyd's remark, Low, *Edward Gibbon*, 161, quoting letters by Holroyd in the British Museum.
2. M. 151. The story of Gibbon's romance has been told repeatedly and in many ways. The best accounts are those by Bonnard, JB. app. II; by Norton, L. app. II; and by Low, *Edward Gibbon*, chaps. 6, 10, and 11.
3. JA. 6; Norton in L. I, 396; Bonnard in JB. 284–5.
4. L. I, 91.
5. L. I, 92–93.
6. L. I, 94–95.
7. L. I, 106; M. 239.
8. JA. 6.

9. Cotter Morison, *Gibbon*, 31.
10. JB. 51–52.
11. L. I, 109 n.
12. M. 239.
13. JB. 52.
14. DF. I, 92.
15. JA. 83.
16. M. 159, 244; JA. 63.
17. M. 205; Hill, 295; MG. 106.
18. JB. 225, 237–8, 247–8; L. I, 177.
19. Quoted by Hill, 336–7.

CHAPTER FOUR

1. Keynes, *The Library of Edward Gibbon*, 70.
2. M. 21.
3. M. 83; but cf. note by Low, JA. li, citing R. L. Poole in *Oxford Magazine*, Nov. 1913.
4. M. 86; but cf. Sheffield's note, MW. I, 62. For Parsons's influence see E. J. Oliver, *Gibbon and Rome* (1958), 47–48, 56.
5. M. 87.
6. Gibbon was connected with the Actons by what he called a 'triple alliance'. His paternal grandmother was a Katharine Acton; her father had married Hester Gibbon, widow of Matthew Gibbon; and Elizabeth Gibbon, Hester's daughter by her first marriage and the first Edward Gibbon's sister, had married Sir Whitmore Acton. One of the Actons — a younger son of a younger son and a cousin of the second Edward Gibbon — studied medicine in France, married a French woman, became a Catholic, and settled in Besançon in the 1730s; another became a Catholic and settled in Italy. John Acton, the doctor's son, entered the service of the King of the Two Sicilies, and was his prime minister for several years before Napoleon expelled him. One of John's sons studied at Cambridge, entered the Roman Catholic priesthood, and eventually became a cardinal; another son was the father of Lord Acton, a Cambridge professor, and one of the leading historians of his day.
7. Hill, 71 n. 5.
8. M. 136 n.
9. MW. I, 83 n.
10. L. I, 3; MW. I, 85 n.
11. M. 87, 89, 129, 137.
12. JA. 94; M. 249.

13. MW. I, 92 n.
14. G. de Beer, in MG. 33.
15. JC. 49; MW. III, 273 and n., 508; M. 145, 237.
16. MW. IV, 414, V, 53–54.
17. L. I, 44; MW. I, 485.
18. M. 143.
19. JA. 129–30; DF. VII, 196 n., 146 n.
20. It is quite possible that, after the lapse of thirty years, Gibbon's memory failed him here, causing him to substitute Grotius for Hume. While at Lausanne Gibbon had read some of Grotius's political treatises, which he occasionally cites in *The Decline and Fall*, but only in this one passage of the Memoirs and once in the History (DF. II, 8, n. 17) does he refer directly to the *De Veritate*. In an early passage of the *Essai* (p. 21), written in 1758 while Gibbon was still in Lausanne, he praises Grotius highly though briefly, saying that he 'combated ignorance and superstition and softened the horrors of war'. I can detect no further trace of Grotius's influence in the *Essai*, though that of Hume's *Natural History of Religion* is easily discernible throughout its later pages. In a 'Dissertation sur les poids' (JA. 10), written in 1759, Gibbon gives a general reference (MW. V, 148) to Hume's *Philosophical Essays*, in which volume the 'Essay on Miracles' appeared. Hume certainly would be as apt as Grotius to lead his readers to make 'a regular tryal of the evidence of Christianity' (M. 249).
21. JB. 24; JC. 159.
22. JB. 30, 222; L. I, 329.
23. JB. 239.
24. M. 262.
25. Porson accused Gibbon of calling Jesus an impostor, but the Cambridge scholar obviously had misread Gibbon's note, DF. I, 328, n. 71, which applies the epithet, not to Jesus but to Apollonius of Tyana. Porson quoted by Hill, 336.
26. DF. V, 105.
27. DF. VII, 321; M. 285; L. III, 216.
28. DF. VI, 131, 134.
29. L. I, 105; II, 52, 392.
30. L. II, 17.
31. L. III, 118.
32. Quoted by Hill, 336.
33. M. 316.
34. Sheffield Papers in Yale Library, III.
35. J. H. Newman, *The Development of Christian Doctrine* (ed. Harrold, 1949), 7.

CHAPTER FIVE

1. M. 11, 17.
2. M. 40, 294.
3. MW. I, 80 n.
4. M. 142; MW. I, 436–55; IV, 92 n.
5. MW. III, 206–22 (in English translation; original French version in MW. 1st edn. (1796), II, 246–62).
6. L. Junod (ed.), in MG. 123–41.
7. Bonnard, in JB. app. I, 273–80; Junod, MG. 115.
8. M. 30–31.
9. L. I, 124. The hope of being 'the instrument of some good to my country' is not one of the eight reasons listed by Sir Lewis Namier, *The Structure of Politics*, for which men went to Parliament in the eighteenth century.
10. L. I, 123–6; JA. 10.
11. JA. 23, 242–4.
12. L. I, 362, 371, 377.
13. L. II, 31–32; Dorothea Gibbon papers at Yale, III, fo. 17.
14. L. II, 34, 63.
15. JA. 145; L. II, 61, 66.
16. Thomas Hutchinson, *Diary and Letters* (1885–6), I, 362, 472; L. II, 51, 57, 59.
17. L. II, 150.
18. M. 314; L. II, 157.
19. L. II, 167; Horace Walpole, *Last Journals*, II, 166.
20. L. II, 167–9, 252.
21. L. II, 140, 176; Low, 275–6.
22. L. II, 200, 202, 204, 209.
23. L. II, 222.
24. Sheffield Papers at Yale, D, fo. 16; for the text of Gibbon's *Mémoire*, see MW. V, 1–34.
25. Walpole, *Last Journals*, II, 464.
26. Norton, *Bibliography*, 28.
27. L. II, 240, 241, 254, and others.
28. L. II, 403; M. 321. Sheffield, too, was of the opinion that Gibbon had been treated most unjustly by members of the opposition. See his footnote in the Memoirs, MW. I, 236.
29. *Parliamentary History*, XXI, 368–74.
30. L. II, 242, 248; Eliot's letter has not been published; it is in the British Museum, Add. MS. 34886, fos. 111–12.
31. L. II, 250, 270 and n. Gibbon's critics sometimes make much of a passage in a letter he wrote to Deyverdun on 20 May 1783.

'You have not forgotten that I entered parliament without patriotism and without ambition, and that all my hopes were limited to a comfortable and honest place on the Board of Trade' (L. II, 327). This statement was certainly true for the seat of Lymington, but it was not true for that of Liskeard. In fact Eliot reminded Gibbon, in the letter explaining why he would not nominate him again for Liskeard, that in their discussions in 1774 he (Gibbon) had declared that he 'had no Lucrative view'. British Museum, Add. MS. 34886, fo. 111.

32. Walpole, *Last Journals*, II, 378; *Parl. Hist.* XXI, 237.

33. In his edition of Gibbon's Memoirs, Birkbeck Hill copied out the two offending passages (p. 319) and reminded his readers that on 14 July 1791, some five or six months after Gibbon wrote (but did not publish) this passage in his Memoirs, 'the magistrates of Birmingham went to sleep while a Church and King mob burnt down his [Priestley's] house and chapel. . . . The magistrates did not wake up until the mob "expanded their views," and began to plunder indiscriminately' (p. 320).

34. L. III, 25, 61, 34.

35. L. III, 44.

36. Sheffield's addition to Gibbon's Memoirs, MW. I, 328; M. 152; L. III, 288.

37. L. III, 318; Sheffield's reply is given in Prothero, *Private Letters of Edward Gibbon*, II, 374: 'As for you, you are a damned, unworthy, temporizing son of a bitch, and shall only be deemed a renegado Englishman in future.'

38. L. II, 395.

39. M. 342–3.

40. L. III, 210, 216, 258.

41. M. 342 n.

42. MW. I, 328–9.

43. L. II, 261, 266, 293, 305; III, 18.

44. L. II, 32.

45. L. II, 248; III, 123–4; M. 420–4.

46. L. III, 196.

47. MW. I, 426–7.

CHAPTER SIX

1. MW. I, 433–530; III, 150–69; IV, 1–93; V, 66–169.

2. MW. IV, 15, 17; for a careful study of the *Essai*, see G. Bonnard, 'Gibbon's *Essai sur l'étude de la littèrature*', in *English Studies*, XXXII (1951), 145–53.

3. MW. IV, 32–37.
4. M. 164.
5. Christopher Dawson, 'Gibbon', in *Proceedings of the British Academy* (1934), 159.
6. JA. 9, 42, 103; cf. 246.
7. JA. 24, 30, 102.
8. JA. 104.
9. L. I, 148, 153–4.
10. MW. IV, 229.
11. JB. 90, 169.
12. MW. IV, 157–326.
13. JB. 211, 213; JC. 122, 156.
14. JB. 168, 241.
15. L. I, 184; M. 302.
16. MW. IV, 467–514; JA. 32; JB. 167; M. 283.
17. L. I, 327–39; MW. II, 83–94.
18. See my 'The Theory of the Four Monarchies: Opposition History under the Roman Empire', in *Classical Philology*, XXXV (1940), 1–27.
19. See Wallace K. Ferguson, *The Renaissance in Historical Thought*.

CHAPTER SEVEN

1. M. 411.
2. JA. 163; DF. I, 138; III, 50; V, 141; MW. IV, 588.
3. DF. I, xxxix; chap. 49; V, 261 ff.; I, 508 (note by Bury).
4. DF. III, 283, n. 88; MW. III, 1–55.
5. MW. III, 31, 29, 25 (cf. DF. I, 73).
6. DF. IV, 172–81; M. 324 n. When Gibbon underlined the word *late* he showed that he was writing after Louis XVI had been deposed (21 September 1792), but before his execution (21 January 1793). For Louis's rejection of Gibbon see Namier and Brooke, *The History of Parliament*, II, 497.
7. L. II, 30. Cadell also published the famous works of Robertson, Hume, Blackstone, Johnson, and Adam Smith.
8. L. II, 81, 105.
9. Norton, *Bibliography*, 37–38; L. II, 116. When Gibbon told his stepmother of this Irish edition, she inquired, 'Do you understand it?' supposing that it was in the Irish language.
10. DF. I, 85–86.
11. DF. I, 7, 9; M. 261.
12. DF. I, 40, 36.

13. DF. I, 31.
14. MW. I, 204; DF. IV, 178.
15. DF. I, 65–79, 86.
16. JA. 71–75.
17. DF. I, 10; Montesquieu, *Considérations*, chaps, 2–3.
18. DF. I, 137.
19. DF. I, 63–64.
20. For the various attacks upon Gibbon, see Norton, *Bibliography*, 78–93 and 233–49; and S. T. McCloy, *Gibbon's Antagonism to Christianity and the Discussions that it has provoked.*
21. L. II, 112, but cf. M. 315.
22. DF. II, 456–504, esp. 486–9, 502.
23. DF. III, 372–3, 506–7.
24. *Parliamentary Register*, V, 119.
25. D. D. Wallace, *The Life of Henry Laurens* (1915), 381.
26. L. II, 370.
27. DF. I, xli.
28. DF. IV, 470–1.

CHAPTER EIGHT

1. L. I, 44; MW. II, 17; Junod, 131–2.
2. DF. I, 64.
3. DF. III, 507.
4. DF. III, 450.
5. M. 311.
6. MW. IV, 517; L. III, 159.

INDEX

Printed by Richard Clay (The Chaucer Press), Ltd.,
Bungay, Suffolk